The Mostly Indian Batch Cookbook

Easy and adaptable recipes from India and beyond, to fill your freezer and feed your soul. For vegans, vegetarians, and omnivores.

Acknowledgements

Before I start, I want to thank my wonderful mum for her expertise and encouragement. I would not be the woman or cook I am today without you. Thank you also to my husband for being such a willing taste-tester and kitchen assistant, for unwavering belief in me, and for his support in every way.

Thank you to everyone who followed my recipes initially, starting this whole process. This would not have happened without you.

And finally, thank you to anyone who has bought this book. I hope it gives you joy and many excellent dinners for years to come.

In memory of my grandfather Surjit 'Serge' Singh, who is fondly remembered through his recipes.

About this book

This book was written during the pandemic and subsequent lockdown of 2020, which fundamentally shifted a lot of the ways we thought about food. Food shortages saw people think about how they could eat healthily and creatively with what was available by cooking in batches and using long-lasting ingredients. This book focuses on South Asian cuisine (particularly the recipes I grew up with) and contains nutritious recipes made from easily sourced ingredients that are often found tinned, dried, frozen, or can be substituted. It is inclusive of all budgets and dietary requirements, open to any level of cooking skill, and has an emphasis on meals that can be cooked in bulk and preserved.

This book is primarily concerned with South Asian cuisine (though there are a few exceptions) as:

1) Personally, it is wonderful comfort food that I grew up with.

2) Curries are easy to learn and adapt once you know the basics. Many of these recipes can be altered to be meat based, vegetarian, or vegan and there are detailed instructions on how to do this.

3) If you do it right, curries are cheap, healthy, keep well in the fridge and freezer, and small amounts of ingredients go a long way.

4) There is so much variety, from simple quick midweek meals to outstanding dinner party dishes.

If you are a novice cook, there are introductory chapters to guide you through the basic essentials of stocking a pantry and kitchen, as well as details on some other appliances and ingredients you may wish to expand to at a later date.

For the more experienced chefs, the sheer number of recipes will provide you with plenty of information as you expand your repertoire and learn restaurant-quality meals, including authentic versions of popular favourites such as Biryani, Rogan Josh, and Vindaloo as well as Indian home cooking from my own family recipes like the Moong Dal, which was always on the menu at my grandparent's house, or the Kebabs we traditionally have over Christmas. I have also included some of my favourite snack food dishes to have in India, like the Punjabi Chole, Aloo Chaat, and the ever unbeatable Pakoras and Samosas.

Every recipe has detailed, simple to follow, and tried and tested instructions for a variety of dishes that can all be easily replicated. Containing mainly flexitarian recipes that can be adjusted for all dietary requirements, and with extensive substitution suggestions, this is a book for all levels of culinary skill and confidence. Also listed within each recipe are both the minimum ingredients needed to replicate the dish as well as optional (but recommended!) additions, depending on what you have available. If you have everything, even better, but the minimum ingredients will still make fantastic and authentic meals.

Part beginner's guide to the kitchen and South Asian food, and part recipe book, all recipes contained within these pages were collected, researched, replicated, and photographed within my own kitchen during the 2020 lockdown. I hope you enjoy this book as much as I did the cooking and writing!

Kay

About the Author

Kathryn 'Kay' Singh BEM is a passionate home cook and multi-award-winning playwright, writer, researcher, and arts facilitator. She is of Indian and Scottish descent, and in 2020 was awarded a BEM in The New Year Honours List for 'Services to the Arts and Asian community in Scotland'. She currently lives in Glasgow with her husband.

Contents

Basics **9**

The ultimate beginner's guide to the kitchen 10

Kitchen equipment 10

Storage equipment 12

Spices and Herbs 12

Things to have in the freezer 14

Things to have in the cupboard 15

The ultimate beginner's guide to Dal 17

Garam Masala 26

Panch Phoran 26

Basic Curry Sauce 28

Jeera Rice 31

Chapatis 32

Soups **34**

Tomato Soup 34

Minestrone Soup 36

Lentil and Vegetable Soup 39

Carrot, Ginger, Chilli, Coriander, and Turmeric Soup 41

Scotch Broth 43

Creamy Spicy Vegan Butternut Squash and Lentil Soup 45

Pea Soup (Ham optional) 47

Leek and Potato Soup 49

Winter Vegetable Soup 50

Jewish Penicillin (Chicken and Rice/Chicken Noodle Soup) 53

Mulligatawny 'Pepper Water' Soup 57

Spanish style meatball and bean stew 60

Chutneys, Pickles, and Sauces 62

Green Chutney 63

Tomato Chutney 65

Tamarind Chutney 66

Raita 69

Spicy Onions 71

Snacks and Starters 73

Chai: A proper cup of desi chai 74

Kebabs 76

Vegan Kebabs 78

Grilled Cheese Naan 82

Aloo Saag Pakora 84

Samosas 87

Aloo Chaat 90

Malaysian Satay 92

Chana Aloo Chaat 93

Bread Omelette 97

Nargis Kebab (The Indian Scotch Egg) 99

Lassi (Yoghurt smoothie) 102

Vegetarian/Vegan 104

Aloo Gobi/Mixed Vegetable Curry 105

Restaurant-style Tadka Dal 109

Super easy and quick chana saag 112

Dal Makhani 114

Palak Paneer 118

Rajma Chawal 122

Mattar Paneer 125

Moong Dal 128

Saag Aloo 131

Chana Dal 133
Punjabi Chole 135
Sweet and creamy coconut vegan dal 138
Jeera Aloo 141
Egg Curry 143
Fijian Potatoes 145
Flexitarian 148
Tandoori/Tikka/Tikka Masala 149
Korma 153
Jalfrezi 156
Biryani 159
Dum Curry 163
Keema Mattar 165
Achari 167
Rogan Josh 169
Bhuna 172
Madras 174
Pathia 177
Vindaloo 180
Desserts/Sweets 182
Kheer (Rice Pudding) 183
Chai Masala Cupcakes And Buttercream Icing 185
Anzac Biscuits 187
Dream Bars 189

Basics

This book contains delicious, nutritious recipes made with easily sourced ingredients. Most of these recipes are designed to be cooked in bulk and frozen for use at a later date, but there are also a few treats and snacks to be put together at the time. The guides and recipes I've put together will help you build confidence in cooking both budget-friendly restaurant-style meals and traditional home recipes.

This section contains detailed information on how to prepare your kitchen for South Asian cuisine and cooking in bulk, and lists the various spices and equipment that will be used for the recipes in this book. I have often added the Hindi names for a lot of the ingredients as this is how I was raised to be familiar with them.

The following parts of this book are things that I normally have in my cupboards and freezer. I have adapted this list slightly for different budgets, and for cooking in bulk. I firmly believe having a few extra ingredients in the pantry and portions in the freezer is never a bad thing. Personally, I try to have at least a few portions of main and side dishes in the freezer, for the days when I can't be bothered but still want a nice cooked meal. Takeaways aren't always the healthiest, and the cost can add up quickly. Also, with these delicious recipes, many of which can be stored for any time you want, I promise that you won't miss them!

The ultimate beginner's guide to the kitchen

Kitchen equipment

I have kept these recipes as simple as possible. You will be able to make everything in this book so long as you have:

- A large pot that can be used on the stove (for most of the soups and curries).
- A roasting tin or baking tray with either a lid or aluminum foil (for curries cooked or finished in the oven).
- A large wooden or plastic spoon to stir your dishes as they cook (wood is great as it doesn't get too hot, but it is porous so needs to be cleaned and dried to prevent from absorbing smells. Plastic also works but you need to be careful not to leave spoons in the pot as they can melt. Both will not scratch your pots).
- Oven gloves and/or tea towels to protect your hands from heat when moving pots and serving.
- A serving spoon or ladle for soups and curries.
- A multipurpose kitchen knife.
- A chopping board.
- A colander for rinsing rice.
- A sieve for straining out stock, rinsing rice and lentils, or sifting out whole spices from chai.
- A cup to measure ingredients, I use a standard mug as most of the recipes are proportional.
- A teaspoon and tablespoon for measuring spices.
- A vegetable peeler for potatoes and carrots (You could use a knife, but peelers are generally inexpensive, make life a lot easier, and there tends to be less waste).
- A grater for fresh ginger, and some vegetables for soup.

- Scales for baking recipes and/or measuring ingredients. (I generally use mugs and spoons to measure in the kitchen, apart from when baking, as most of these recipes are proportional).
- Rolling pin for dough, as used in the samosa recipe and for chapatis.
- A mortar and pestle for making chutneys and spice mixes by hand.
- A blender that can make chutneys quickly, lassi (a yoghurt-based drink included in the book), and creamed soups.
- A spice grinder if you wish to make your own spice mixtures and curry powders quickly and with less effort, though many of these are already easily found in shops and online. You can also use a pestle and mortar though this will take more time.

Other things that may be useful are:

- An oven-safe sauté pan with a lid, casserole pot, Dutch oven, or any hob to oven dish with a lid as these can be used for both stovetop and oven cooking. If there is one pot you can buy, something like this is perfect as you can use it for everything. These do tend to vary a lot in price, but personally I was given one on the cheapest end of the scale 10 years ago and I have only just had to replace it after almost daily use.
- A food processor for chopping vegetables (you can also buy combined food processors and blenders).
- A pressure cooker for cooking lentils quickly.
- Rice cooker for making rice without needing stovetop space.

Storage equipment

- Freezer bags (preferably ones with the zip lock, if using tie bags ensure you remove all of the air and tie them very tightly).
- Sealable plastic tubs with lids for a more environmentally friendly approach.

I prefer to use reusable plastic tubs as they are better for the environment, both ingredients and portions keep better, and there is no leakage of sauces or smells if you are storing things like soup or garlic. These are also excellent for storing spices and ingredients both in the cupboard and in the fridge and freezer so I would recommend a set of various sizes. For example, 3-5 litre boxes are great for storing lentils, pulses and cereals, 0.5-1 litre sizes are great for storing portions, and the smallest boxes can be used for freezing and storing smaller portions, side dishes, garlic, ginger, chillies, and herbs.

Spices and Herbs

Please note I tend to use ground spices as they are the easiest to find, store and cook with. You can use whole spices if you wish, and some recipes work best with a mixture. You can also make your own spice masalas or mixtures, though these do tend to be found in most supermarkets, online, and in any Asian grocer. The best way to store spices is in a traditional masala dabba (several small sealed containers within a larger steel container), but failing that, small sealable plastic tubs will work perfectly. Certain supermarkets have also started to stock resealable packs, which are fantastic.

- Must-haves for Indian food are cumin (jeera), coriander (dhaniya), turmeric (haldi), garam masala, chilli powder, and salt. If you are on a budget or unsure these are the bare necessities, and many recipes in this book can be made just using these. My favourite salt to use is pink salt or Himalayan salt, it is quite expensive in supermarkets but can be found cheaply online and in your local Asian food shop.

- There are also several different curry powders and spice packets that can be found both at your local supermarket and Asian food shop. I would recommend having at least one generic curry powder in your spice cupboard, such as a Madras curry powder, as these are very versatile and can be used to make dishes quickly. Curry powders tend to have different levels of heat advertised on them and can generally be used with any curry dish, and spice mixture packets usually have a picture and name the specific dish they are for.

- Less essential but still great to have are fenugreek (methi) that works well with most vegetable curries, panch phoran (a spice mix that can be used as curry powder and for making pickles), dried mango powder (amchur), fennel (saumf), mustard seeds, cardamom, cinnamon, cloves, and tamarind paste.

- Ginger garlic paste is ideal for cooking curries, as you spend less time prepping ginger and garlic, plus the paste lasts for ages unopened, three weeks in the fridge after being opened, and can be frozen in sealable plastic tubs and freezer bags. Never run out of fresh garlic or ginger again!

- Note that if you, or those you are cooking for, do not eat onions you can replace onion with fresh fennel or a tbsp of fennel seeds, or two tsps of ground fennel. If you do not eat garlic, you can replace this with a teaspoon or two of ground asafoetida, also called hing.

- Oregano, basil, rosemary, thyme, and sage for soups and stews.

- Bouquet garni for easy and tasty soups.

- Smoked paprika and cayenne pepper give warmth and a meaty flavour to vegetarian dishes such as soups and stews.

Things to have in the freezer

- Frozen vegetables (especially peas, carrots, peppers, cauliflower and spinach).
- Chopped onions, in freezer bags or sealable plastic tubs.
- Garlic, in freezer bags or sealable plastic tubs (whole cloves for roasting, chopped or minced for curries).
- Ginger, in freezer bags or sealable plastic tubs (peeled, minced or grated).
- Chillies, in freezer bags or sealable plastic tubs (can be frozen chopped or whole, as long as you remove the stems and any signs of rot).
- Mince, your preferred flavour is fine be it vegetarian/vegan replacement, chicken, turkey, lamb, or beef. If you are freezing, try to stack the mince flat in freezer bags with a zip lock as this is the most efficient use of space.
- Chicken breasts, tofu, or paneer. Store in freezer bags. Paneer should generally be defrosted before using, simply keep it in the packet or freezer bag and place in hot water to defrost. This method also works for meat and vegetables. Careful the water is not too hot though, you only want to defrost what is in the bag, not cook it.
- Chopped herbs in freezer bags or sealable plastic tubs (especially parsley, coriander, and mint). These can be thrown into soups and curries for the last few minutes of cooking to add a freshness to the flavour.
- Basic soup mixes. You can buy these in pre-prepared packs at the supermarket but they generally consist of chopped onion, celery, carrot, turnip, and leek. You can also make your own by chopping up vegetables then freezing them in the same sealed plastic bag or tub, then use this as a base for most soups.

Things to have in the cupboard

- Oil (vegetable oil is ideal for most of the recipes, ghee is wonderful in Indian food but not vegan).

- Stock cubes, the plainer the better. Add these to boiling water, see the packet for exact instructions and amounts, then add to soups and curries for more depth of flavour. You can also substitute with boiling water and a few pinches of salt to taste.

- Tinned tomatoes, with no added herbs or spices. I use the 400g/14oz cans for the recipes in this book.

- Tomato puree.

- Rice, personally I prefer basmati rice, and it is cheaper to buy in bulk.

- Any types of lentils and pulses, for example, chickpeas (chana either whole in a tin or split and dry), pigeon pea (toor), red lentil (masoor), kidney beans (rajma) in a tin or dried, or my personal favourite, whole green gram (moong). There is a deeper dive into types of lentils and dals, basic storage principles, and also several images in the book as a guide. This book contains recipes for each of these dals and more, and many can be substituted.

- Pasta (for soups, the smaller the better).

- Pickles/chutneys are an excellent way to add a bit of extra flavour in your cooking, and are generally cheap and last for months. Popular versions for curries include mint chutney, mango pickle/chutney, lime pickle, chilli pickle, as well as mixed pickles. Most of these can be found in supermarkets, but you may need to venture out to your local Asian food store or look online. There are a few recipes for sauces/chutneys in this book, and some recipes use them as ingredients.

- Cider vinegar or white wine vinegar is used in some of the recipes.

- Lemon juice can be used as a substitute for vinegar and to take the edge of anything too oily. This is also perfect squeezed over vegetarian curry and dal before serving.

The ultimate beginner's guide to Dal

If you don't know much about Indian cooking, or have never even looked at a lentil, here's the place to start! In this section I will be going through some frequently asked questions, descriptions of some of the most popular dals, and the basics on how to store and cook.

What is dal?
Also spelled dhal, dahl, or daal, it is a catch-all term for pulses, lentils and beans in South Asia. More often used as a description for a soup-like curried dish made from these as the main ingredient.

So, is it like lentil soup then?
Yes, basically. With a few modifications.

What's so great about dal?
What isn't? It is tasty, cheap, a little bit goes a long way, it stores well, is easy to make, and incredibly rich in proteins and vitamins. There is a reason it is the staple of most South Asian cooking!

What are the main types of dal, and what is the difference between them?
Ok, here's a breakdown of some of the main types of dal, what they are used for and what you can substitute them with. Generally, each dal comes in whole and split versions. An easy way to tell if they are whole is that they will be round, if they are split they will look like they have been split in half.

- Toor (split pigeon pea), split moong (yellow lentils), chana (split chickpeas) can often be used together in the same dal or used interchangeably. Once cooked, they have a creamy texture and delicate flavour that picks up garlic and lighter spice mixes. You can also add a little bit of urid/urad (black gram), whole or split, to them for a bit of added texture and flavour. Masoor (red lentil) can be a little bit bland on its own, but adds a nice balance, texture and colour to these dals above.

- Whole urid dal (black gram lentils) used on their own have a savoury, peppery taste that picks up ginger, tomato and chilli spectacularly and have a bit more texture. This dal also comes in a variety of forms, split and unskinned, split and skinned, whole and skinned etc, each with a slightly different texture and flavour. These can be cooked with rajma (kidney beans) for a creamier dal.

- Whole hare mung (green gram lentil) are almost in between the two. They still have a creamy texture but really pick up any flavour you cook them with, especially chilli. These can be mixed with lobia (black-eyed peas) for a little variety in texture.

- Whole chana (chickpeas) are really easy to cook from a can, no need to soak, and have an excellent texture. These can be easily mixed with potato and/or chopped frozen spinach as well.

Split versions are usually easier to digest, cook in a much shorter period of time, and do not need soaking.

Wait, hang on, I need to soak it?

Well, depends. Generally, whole versions of the lentils require soaking for a few hours before cooking, or some even overnight. This makes the dal easier to digest and speeds up cooking times by half. If you use boiling water, you don't need to soak them for as long. If you are using a slow cooker or pressure cooker, or you use split versions rather than whole, you do not need to soak them though many people like to for about 20 minutes as it still speeds up cooking time. All dal should be thoroughly rinsed and drained before cooking.

How do I cook it?

There are so many different ways of preparing this dish, depending on region, culture and even individual family groups. A really simple way is to cook the lentils separately in water with a bit of salt and turmeric until tender, while doing this fry your onions, spices, chilli, garlic, ginger, salt and tomato together. Then skim off any foam that might have appeared on top of the dal, add the fried mixture and dal together, then cook for a further 10 minutes or until the lentils are at the consistency you like. This book has plenty of dal and lentil-based recipes with very detailed instructions including Chana Masala, Moong Dal, Tadka Dal, and Dal Makhani, as well as others.

Where can I buy dal?

You can find the most common types of dal in most supermarkets, though you may have to go to your local Asian food store or online retailers for others. I have given both the English and Hindi/Urdu terms to make it easier for you to find them.

How do I store it?

Dried dal or tinned beans that you buy in shops keep for ages in the cupboard. You can keep dried dal in the plastic bags they come in as often these are resealable, or keep them in a freezer bag, or store them in sealed plastic containers. Once cooked, dal keeps in the fridge for three days. Freeze dal on the day of cooking in sealed plastic containers, or freezer bags, and dal can keep for months.

Is there anything else I can add to dal?

Yes, of course, experiment! Some people add a bit of spinach, or potato, or even lamb or chicken. If adding meat, I would chop it up and brown it first before adding to the dal and simmer for at least 30 minutes, and check everything is cooked through before serving.

Chana (split chickpea lentil)

Toor (split pigeon pea)

Masoor (split red lentil)

Urid (black lentil, split but not deshelled)

Moong (whole green gram lentil)

Lobia (black-eyed peas)

Garam Masala

Garam Masala is predominantly used in Northern Indian cooking, and is widely found in shops. It translates to 'hot mixture' and usually contains fennel (saunf), black and white peppercorns (kali/safed mirch), cloves (laung), cinnamon or cassia bark (darchini), mace - outer covering of nutmeg - (javitri), black and green cardamom pods (elaichi), cumin seeds (jeera), and coriander seeds (dhania). It has a warming and fragrant flavour, and is mostly found powdered.

Panch Phoran

Panch phoron originates from Bangladesh and Southern Nepal. It can be found online and in your local Asian supermarket. It translates to 'five spices' which are cumin seeds, fenugreek seeds, fennel seeds, mustard seeds, and kalongi or nigella seeds. Unlike a lot of spice mixes in India it is not ground but kept whole. These seeds are also often used when making chutneys and pickles. It has a spicy and tangy flavour.

Basic Curry Sauce

Here is a simple recipe for making a large batch of curry sauce, that you can then freeze and use as a base in the future. When using, simply defrost a portion of the sauce in the microwave or a pan, then add your fresh or frozen veg with a little water and salt, then simply heat up and simmer until everything is cooked through and you get your desired consistency. For lentils simply add the sauce to a pan, add boiling water and a few pinches of salt, and add the lentils. Make sure the lentils are covered, bring everything to a boil, then simmer for 40 minutes until you get the consistency you want, and the lentils are cooked through. This will take less time for canned lentils. For a meat curry, brown your meat first in a little oil for a few minutes, then add the sauce with a little water and salt, then heat up and reduce to your desired consistency. This recipe makes 3-4 large amounts of sauce for freezing, that can each be used to make 3-4 portions of curry, so in total, you should get 12-16 servings from this recipe depending on what ingredients you use and size of servings.

This is a simple sauce that can be used with anything, you may wish to add cinnamon/cloves for a more aromatic curry on the reheat, or add tamarind for a tangy flavour, or add more chilli if you like your food hot. Honestly, whatever works for you. I often choose to make this as simple as possible, then jazz it up depending on how I am feeling on the day of using it as a base, or keep it as it is.

INGREDIENTS:

-1 kg of onions, chopped
-4 tinned tomatoes
-3 heaped tbsps of minced ginger and garlic
-4 heaped tsps of salt
-4 heaped tsps of turmeric
-4 heaped tsps of ground coriander
-4 heaped tsps of ground cumin
-4 heaped tsps of garam masala
-A few tbsps of oil or ghee

Optional: I like to add two tsps of amchur (powdered dried unripe mango), two tsps of red chilli powder and a few bay leaves as they also go with anything. You can also put in fresh chillies.

METHOD:

-Add a layer of oil to the pan and heat up to a medium heat, then add the onions. You want to cook these for a while so that they soften and turn golden rather than brown.
-Add your salt, ginger and garlic, and fresh chillies if using. Cook for a further few minutes. Add more oil if needed.
-Add in your ground spices and stir, making sure not to burn them on the bottom of the pan. Lower the heat if necessary or add more oil. The longer you cook the onions and spices, the tastier this will be. There should be a paste-like consistency when finished that does not stick to the bottom of the pan.
-Add tomatoes and keep this simmering as long as possible, the consistency will continue to thicken as the onions and tomatoes break down. Taste and see if there is anything you need to add more of. You should aim for quite an intense flavour as when using this as a base you will add some stock or salt and water.
-When finished allow to cool, put in a food processor if you wish, or simply divide into 3 or 4 batches and freeze for an easy meal at a later date!

Jeera Rice

This is the standard recipe for rice in my house. With just a few tweaks you can make boiled rice into a very tasty and pretty accompaniment to any dish.

INGREDIENTS:

-1 ½ cups of rice (preferably Basmati) per two people
-4 to 5 cups of water (enough for the rice to expand properly)
-1 tsp of cumin seeds (you can use ground cumin but cumin seeds have a lovely visual effect)
-1 tsp of turmeric
-Salt to taste

METHOD:

-Place your rice in a sieve and rinse through a few times with cold water.
-Bring a pot of water to the boil.
-Add a tsp of salt, more if you like your rice salty.
-Add in you other spices.
-Add in your rice, stir once at the beginning to ensure that the rice is covered, then every 5 minutes for fifteen minutes, or however long it says on the back of the packet.
-Drain your rice, if it looks a little stodgy rinse it again with boiling water.
-Enjoy!

Chapatis

Chapatis are difficult to get the knack of, as the exact amount needed for each ingredient will vary greatly depending on what flour you are using, and even the humidity of where you live. It is worth getting the knack of them though, if you have the time and inclination. Below are the rough proportions and method. I use a mug to measure out my ingredients - the proportions are more important than the exact amount.

INGREDIENTS:

-2 cups of wholemeal flour, you can also use a mix of white flour and wholemeal flour, or chapatti flour of you can find it
-3/4 cup of water
-1/2 a tsp of salt
-1 tbsp of oil

METHOD:

-Put the flour in a bowl and add the oil and salt, stir this in until you get the consistency of breadcrumbs.
-Add the water in slowly, stirring and kneading throughout until you get a soft dough that is not too sticky.
-Divide this into balls, then roll and flatten the balls as much as possible until you have thin circles.
-Place on a hot pan for thirty to forty seconds, then flip over and press down. The chapatti should start to inflate. If you have a gas hob, place this on a gas flame for a few seconds to inflate more. If they do not inflate, the dough is too thick, if they turn crispy the dough is too thin.
-Enjoy!

Soups

If you are not a confident cook, want to eat a bit healthier, eat on a budget, or start bulk cooking, soups are an excellent way to start!

Tomato Soup

This is a wonderfully easy and versatile soup that is ideal for serving as a starter or if you are feeling under the weather. My favourite is to serve this with a grilled cheese naan (the recipe can be found in the snacks/starters section). You can make tomato soup from only an onion and/or celery, a few 400g tins of tomatoes, water, and some salt. However, I like to experiment with different flavours. You can also add in a few frozen peppers for added vegetables, or some fresh or frozen chillies and/or basil. You can also add vegetable stock, and season with salt and smoked paprika to taste. For a more Italian taste, you can season with dried basil, oregano and thyme. For a more Indian flavour, add chillies and/or chilli powder to taste. You can then cook any version of your soup further until it thickens, then freeze for a simple pasta sauce for use at a later date. Or simply freeze as a soup. There are so many possibilities!

INGREDIENTS:

-1 onion and/or 2 stalks of celery and/or a few peppers.
-2 400g tins of tomatoes
-1 litre of vegetable stock, or a litre of water and salt to taste
-Dash of oil
Optional seasoning: basil, oregano, thyme, or paprika and chilli. Bouquet garni and bay leaves also work well with tomatoes

METHOD:

-Fry your finely chopped onions/celery/peppers in oil for at least five minutes on a medium heat until very soft.
-Add in your 400g tins of tomatoes (at least two).
-Add salt and vegetable stock until you get a slightly thinner consistency than you want.
-Add in preferred seasoning to taste.
-Simmer for twenty minutes.
-Serve or further reduce and/or blend for a thicker soup that can be used as a pasta sauce. You can also add cheese to the soup, which will thicken and become creamier.
-Enjoy!

Minestrone Soup

There are many recipes for minestrone out there, in fact, it can be made from whatever you have in the fridge/freezer/cupboard. The name in Italian means "soup- that which is served". Frozen vegetables, tinned tomatoes, and tinned beans work very well. The soup also freezes well. It can contain meat or be vegetarian. Here is a basic one. For a vegetarian version, leave out the pancetta and use vegetable stock, and a bit of smoked paprika works well to give it a deeper flavour.

I like my minestrone to be made with pancetta cubes, which keep for a while and can also be frozen, as this helps give it a really rich flavour. The other secret is to do what the Cajun's call "The Holy Trinity". This means that the onions, celery and peppers are slowly fried in oil until they nearly caramelise, adding yet more depth to the final soup. I also add a handful of diced fennel that I often have frozen as fresh fennel does not keep particularly well and goes brown (oxidises) easily. In fact, I use fennel quite a lot in casseroles and curries, often as a substitute for garlic and/or onion. I also add quite a bit of crushed garlic about half way through cooking the "Holy Trinity" along with diced carrots.

After you add the tomatoes (tinned or fresh) and the stock, I add about half a diced courgette (freeze the other half but dice it first). Some people like to add lots of herbs/basil/bouquet garni but I quite like a sprinkling of dried rosemary, oregano and thyme. If you have a leftover parmesan rind, this can be frozen first then added in at this point for a really tasty soup, just take it out before serving and freezing. Finally, towards the end, a handful of chopped kale/cabbage/green beans (all freeze well) and some tinned beans (borlotti/cannellini/butter).

You can freeze the soup as it is, or freeze without the pasta then add this on the reheat. Smaller pasta freezes better than larger types.

INGREDIENTS:

-1 tbsp butter/oil
-Pancetta (optional), if not using you can add a bit of smoked paprika with the herbs
-1 white onion, chopped
-2 stalks of celery, chopped
-1 red pepper, chopped
-½ a fennel, diced
-½ a courgette, chopped
-2 to 3 garlic cloves, crushed
-4 carrot sticks, peeled and chopped
-Green beans/kale/cabbage, trimmed and cut into 2/3cm pieces
-1 x 400g tin of tomatoes
-1 can of beans (see above), drained and rinsed
-Sprinkling of dried rosemary, oregano and thyme to taste, and/or bay leaves, and/or general Italian herb seasoning (smoked paprika and a pinch of chilli powder can also be added)
-Chicken or vegetable stock (or equivalent bouillon base)
-Parmesan rind (if using)
-Pasta
-Salt and pepper to taste
-Parmesan cheese to serve (optional)

METHOD:

-Fry pancetta (if using), celery, onion and pepper until caramelised. Add fennel if using. Add carrots and garlic.
-Add tinned tomatoes and stock, bring to boil. Add courgette. Add parmesan rind if using. Lower heat.
-Add herbs and salt to taste, cook for 10 minutes.
-Add washed and drained tinned beans. Add chopped kale/cabbage/green beans. Add pasta.
-Serve when pasta is cooked. Remove Parmesan rind.

Lentil and Vegetable Soup

Here is a simple lentil and vegetable soup that you can add bacon to if you wish. I like to use leftover roasted smoked gammon, which is a very cheap and versatile roast that lasts for ages and can be easily frozen. I often have the vegetables pre-chopped together in the freezer, which makes the recipe even easier.

INGREDIENTS:

-1 or 2 onions
-1 tbsp of vegetable oil
-3 cloves of garlic
-3 to 4 finely diced carrots
-3 finely chopped leeks
-1 finely chopped turnip
-A handful or two of red lentils
-1 litre of vegetable stock
-Bouquet garni, or bay leaf, rosemary, basil, thyme and parsley

Optional: Bacon/pancetta/gammon

METHOD:

-In a large pot fry onions in oil with garlic, and bacon/pancetta/gammon if using. Fry until onion is translucent.
-Add chopped leeks, turnip and carrot and fry for a further minute or two. Add lentils.
-Add in 1 litre of vegetable stock. Add bouquet garni, or a bay leaf, and a sprinkling of rosemary, basil thyme and parsley.
-Bring pot to the boil. Put the heat down, taste for any further salt/herbs to be added. Let it simmer for at least 40-50 minutes.
-Enjoy!

Carrot, Ginger, Chilli, Coriander, and Turmeric Soup

This can be made from frozen chopped onion, ginger, coriander, and carrots. You can also make this without the ginger, turmeric or bay leaves. Coconut milk and cream work equally well to give it a nice texture, but it also tastes great without. Very simple and tasty, freezes well, and makes for a great starter or main course. I would also highly recommend when feeling unwell, and this is one I often make if I have a cold as it is very easy to put together from a few frozen bits and pieces, and the ginger is fantastic for soothing a sore throat and unblocking sinuses.

INGREDIENTS:

-750g carrots, grated and chopped finely
-2 chopped onions, white or red
-3 cloves of garlic
-2 inches of grated ginger, or two heaped tsps of ginger paste
-1 or 2 chillies, or 1tsp of chilli powder, to taste
-2 bay leaves
-1 heaped tsp of turmeric
-1 litre of vegetable stock
-1 tbsp of oil
-Salt to taste

METHOD:

-Fry your onions in a little oil for a minute or two, adding a dash of salt to speed up the softening process.
-Add your garlic, ginger, chilli, and turmeric if using. Add bay leaves if using. Stir thoroughly for another minute.

-Add in your carrots and keep cooking until they turn soft, adding a touch more water or oil if the mixture starts to stick to the bottom of the pan. This will take about 10 minutes.
-When the carrots are very nearly cooked but still have a bit of bite, add in a litre of hot vegetable stock.
-Bring to a boil, then simmer for 15-20 minutes. Let it cool slightly and remove bay leaves.
-Add in cream or coconut milk if using, then blend until smooth
-Add in chopped coriander.
-If you wish, garnish with a little more coriander, pepper, and/or crushed chillies if you want more heat.
-Enjoy!

Scotch Broth

I think the beauty of this, as with most traditional rustic cooking, is that you can substitute a lot of the ingredients with whatever you have lying around and/or access to. For this recipe, I use frozen carrots, peas, turnip, and onion, but you can also add or substitute celery, leeks, celeriac, parsnips, fennel, and kale. Whatever works for you! I also use a small handful of pearl barley, which is traditional and my local shop sells it, but you can also use a handful of any split lentils to make this a vegetable and lentil soup (just be aware that the more lentils/barley you add, the thicker the soup will be). Traditionally this would have been made with a little bit of chopped lamb/mutton meat, particularly neck as that is a cheap cut, which you can add with the onions and celery and fry for a few minutes before boiling with the rest of the ingredients. You can also make this with chicken stock and/or chopped meat, or keep it vegetarian or vegan as I did here. If you have bouquet garni or thyme, rosemary, parsley and bay leaves that's great, otherwise, the vegetable or chicken stock can do all the work, or simply add salt and pepper to taste. This is ideal as a stovetop recipe as the soup doesn't need babysitting, and also as a slow cooker recipe. For a slow cooker version just put in all the ingredients and cook on high for 6-8 hours.

INGREDIENTS:

-1 onion
-2 carrots
-1 medium sized turnip
-1 handful of frozen peas
-1 handful of pearl barley
-1 litre of vegetable stock
-Salt and pepper to taste

Optional: herbs, bouquet garni, bay leaves

METHOD:

-Fry the onion, carrots, and celery if using, for a few minutes in either oil or butter. If you are using any meat add this in as well.
-Stir until the vegetables are soft and the meat has begun to brown, then add the rest of the vegetables, and barley or lentils, and stir until they are coated.
-Add in the stock plus any herbs if using, then bring the mixture to a boil.
-Put the heat down and simmer for at least 50 minutes, or until the barley has softened/lentils have cooked through. To be honest the longer this soup simmers, the better. You can just leave this soup to do its own thing, there's no need to stand over the pot.
-Enjoy!

Creamy Spicy Vegan Butternut Squash and Lentil Soup

This is one of my favourite soups to have a few portions of lying around, as it freezes very well and is versatile as a meal by itself or as a starter. It has a delicate yet tasty flavour while also being very filling. If you want a creamy texture to a soup without adding dairy, simply add a finely chopped skinless potato to your soup, simmer until cooked, then blend with a food processor. If you don't have a food processor you can leave out the potato or use a whisk or potato masher. You can also keep the small cubes of potato for a chunky soup.

INGREDIENTS:

-1 finely cubed butternut squash (sweet potato would also work)
-1 finely chopped red onion
-1 finely chopped red pepper
-1 skinned finely chopped potato
-1 cup of split red lentils or pigeon pea
-3 chopped cloves of garlic
-1 tsp of dried and crushed chillies, to taste
-1/2 a tsp of smoked paprika
-1/2 a tsp of cumin (If you don't have paprika, cumin, or chillies a tsp of curry powder and/or chilli powder to taste would work)
-1 litre of water with vegetable stock and/or salt
-1 tbsp of oil

Optional: parsley and pepper to garnish

METHOD:

-Add oil to a pot on a medium heat. Add onion, garlic, and pepper and cook until soft and caramelised.
-Add the butternut squash and/or sweet potato and stir in for a minute.
-Add in stock and stir.
-Add your lentils and spices, stir well.
-Bring to a boil, then lower the heat and simmer for 30-40 minutes.
-Peel and chop a potato into fine cubes, add to the soup and simmer for a further 10 minutes until cooked. Check the consistency of the lentils and potatoes to ensure they are cooked. Check the taste and see if there are any more spices and/or salt to add. If it is too spicy you can add another potato and more salt and water/vegetable stock.
-Once everything is cooked through and you are are happy with the flavours, lower the heat and either use a handheld blender or food processor to get a creamy texture. If you don't have a food processor you can use a whisk or potato masher to mash up the potatoes and lentils.
-Add chopped parsley and black pepper if you wish.
-Enjoy!

Pea Soup (Ham optional)

This is one of the cheapest, quickest, and easiest dishes I have ever made, from just a few ingredients and frozen peas. It keeps well and has such a lovely fresh taste while being surprisingly filling. This works equally well as a meat or vegetarian dish, just garnish with a little mint at the end if you have it, or for a meat version add a bit of bacon or ham and touch of cream at the end. If you want a thicker texture without using cream, add a finely chopped medium-sized potato and cook in the soup before blending. I like to use leftover roasted gammon marinated with garlic, dijon mustard, crushed cloves, honey, and lemon, then drain the juices after cooking the roast to use as stock, then add a little mint and a few chunks of meat at the end.

INGREDIENTS:

-1 white onion, finely chopped
-2 to 3 garlic cloves, crushed then finely chopped
-500g frozen peas
-1 litre of stock, either vegetable for a vegetarian version, chicken, or if using leftover roast ham you can use some of the strained juices as stock

Optional but recommended: A touch of mint, cream to taste, a handful of cooked and chopped bacon, pancetta, ham, or gammon.

METHOD:

-Fry your onion and garlic in a tbsp of oil on a medium heat until the onion softens and you can no longer smell the fresh onion, about 5 minutes.
-If using potato, add this in and fry for a few minutes until it begins to soften.
-Add in your frozen peas and chosen stock, bring to a boil then simmer for 10-15 minutes.
-If using cream, add this in before blending.
-Blend then serve garnished with a touch of mint if you have it for a vegetarian version, or a touch of cream, or a bit of finely chopped bacon/gammon/pancetta, or all of the above.
-Enjoy!

Leek and Potato Soup

If you have a few potatoes that need eating up, leek and potato soup is an excellent way of using them. I often have diced frozen leeks and onion in my freezer, which makes this recipe even easier, and they are ideal for using as a base for a variety of soups.

INGREDIENTS:

-4 potatoes
-4 leeks
-1 onion
-3 garlic cloves, crushed and chopped
-1 litre of vegetable stock
-1 tbsp of oil
-Salt and pepper to taste

Optional: cream, parsley, bouquet garni, or a sprinkling of Italian herb seasoning

METHOD:

-Skin and cube your potatoes then throw them in a pan with oil along with a diced onion, three chopped cloves of garlic, and leeks.
-Fry for a few minutes until they turn soft.
-Add vegetable stock.
-Bring to the boil then simmer for 30-40 minutes, add in some chopped parsley and/or herbs but not too much as it can overpower the soup. -If you are feeling fancy, you can then blend it with milk or cream.
-Add salt and pepper to taste. -Enjoy!

Winter Vegetable Soup

This is a very hearty and filling vegan recipe that is great for adding any frozen vegetables to, and then freezing to use at a later date. I love to have this on its own with crusty bread, and this is a meal in itself.

INGREDIENTS:

-3 leeks, diced
-3 carrots, chopped
-2 cloves of garlic, crushed and chopped
-1 handful of split lentils, either split pigeon pea, split yellow lentils, or split red lentils
-1 white onion, chopped
-2 potatoes, cubed
-1 mug of peas, fresh or frozen
-1 handful of spinach, fresh or frozen
-1 litre of vegetable stock
-Salt and pepper to taste

Seasoning (optional), either bouquet garni, bay leaf, or a sprinkling of rosemary and thyme, parsley

METHOD:

-Fry your onion, leeks, and carrot in oil for a few minutes until they turn soft.
-Add garlic and fry for a further minute, be careful not to burn the garlic.
-Rinse and drain your lentils.
-Add in your lentils and stir for a minute, making sure that they are coated in the oil.
-Add in your vegetable stock and any seasoning you are using.
-Bring to a boil, then lower heat slightly and cook until the lentils soften, about 30 minutes.
-Add in your diced potatoes.
-When the potatoes are nearly cooked, add in your spinach and peas. These will only take a few minutes to cook.
-When everything has cooked through, serve immediately.
-Enjoy!

Jewish Penicillin (Chicken and Rice/Chicken Noodle Soup)

This recipe is very close to my heart and has been passed down the maternal side of my family for several generations. My grandmother, who was of Jewish ancestry on her maternal side, would make this for my mother and her siblings whenever they were unwell, and in turn my mother always made this for me whenever I was ill. To this day she will often deliver a portion to me when I am sick (it freezes brilliantly) as it is the ultimate comfort food, and I swear has mystical healing powers.

This also contains a recipe for chicken stock, which should be made from leftover roast chicken, then can be used as a basis for this and other soups. I generally use stock cubes nowadays but this soup really needs "proper" stock. I never throw away a roasted chicken carcass and even if I don't have time to make the stock then, I freeze the whole carcass (after stripping it of most of the meat) and boil it at a later date. The roasted remains add more flavour due to caramelising of the bones etc. In fact, any roasted meat bones make great stock.

INGREDIENTS FOR STOCK:

-Leftover roast chicken (if you have roasted the chicken with onion and garlic in the cavity, use this in the stock as well)
-1 onion, chopped
-A bunch of celery leaves, chopped

Optional: bay leaf or bouquet garni

INGREDIENTS FOR SOUP:

-3 leeks, sliced (you can also use onion)
-2 sticks of celery, finely diced
-3 carrot sticks, grated
-Handful of parsley
-Handful of pasta, rice, or noodles (I prefer to use either instant noodles, or Vermicelli, or Capellini also known as Angel Hair pasta. If I'm using rice, long grain works best)
-Chicken stock
-Salt to taste
-Pepper to taste

Optional: bay leaf, bouquet garni, herbs.

METHOD:

-For the stock put the chicken in a pan and cover it with water. If you've roasted the chicken with onions and garlic in its cavity, add them as well. Add an onion, carrot and celery leaves (don't throw them away, they freeze really well and are great for stocks). Some people add a bouquet garni or a bay leaf but for this recipe, its secret is the simple flavours. Boil this for as long as you have - the longer the better. When it's done, strain the liquid and use. This also freezes well for use with any chicken recipe. Don't worry if it goes all thick and gelatinous after cooling- this means that it is a really good stock. Sometimes there is a white layer of fat on the top. Don't throw that away, it is very good for frying the base vegetables.

-In a pan, add at least a couple of handfuls of sliced leeks (I often freeze leeks already sliced as they can then be easily used). Add a handful of diced celery (I never get through a whole celery so dice up the stalks and freeze them) and continue to fry slowly until the leeks are translucent. Add a couple of grated carrots (some people like finely diced carrot) and some chopped parsley. Parsley for soups freezes very well and you do not even need to chop it up as it is very brittle when it comes out and breaks up well. Don't use too much as it can overpower the soup. Add the stock and cook until the vegetables are cooked. You may need to add a chicken stock cube or two and some salt. Now, the choice of what carbs to go in. I am always in a dilemma! But, the secret is not too much as the carbs swell and it makes the soup very thick. This is a very thin soup with floating pasta or rice. My personal favourite is Angel Hair pasta or instant noodles but any small pasta or spaghetti broken into small bits will do. The best rice is ordinary long grain rice.

-Add the carbs and cook for another 10/15 minutes. If you want to use up some leftover chicken, put this in as well though it isn't necessary. Season with more salt if needed. Add a little black pepper.

-Enjoy!

Mulligatawny 'Pepper Water' Soup

Easy, versatile, and the original Indian-British 'fusion food'. This is a dish that is a popular staple within the Anglo-Indian community, who are originally descended from British Officers who married local Indian women, and then received a large bonus for having baptised Protestant children. These children would then often grow up to marry other Anglo-Indians, forming a unique minority cultural group that was often Christian, spoke English as a mother tongue, and had Anglo-Centric cultural tastes in dress, music, and food. The name originates from the Tamil words milagay (chilli) or milagu (pepper), and tanni (water). It is said that some British officers stationed in Southern India asked a Tamil chef to make a soup, which didn't have a place in Indian cuisine, and this was the resulting interpretation. It became extremely popular with the British stationed in India, and then was eventually brought over to Britain. In Anglo-Indian communities, it is known as 'Pepper Water'. There are so many variations on this soup, I think it is ideal for throwing in whatever you have lying around, is perfect as a vegetarian or meat soup, and can be made as simple or as complicated as you like. If you want you can add or use cumin, coriander, turmeric, garam masala and chilli powder to flavour this but I only use curry powder, mango chutney, and tamarind. That's it. It should have a sweet and sour taste with an underlying acidity. You can add coconut milk, yoghurt, or cream for a thicker soup, but traditionally this is a thinner watery soup with little chunks of meat or veg.

INGREDIENTS:

-2 white onions
-2 cloves of garlic, if desired
-2 carrots (you can also add/substitute leeks, and celery)
-250g to 400g of veg and/or meat (any meat will work, chicken, lamb, or beef are popular. You can use mince or chunks. Vegetables can include sweet potato, aubergine, mushrooms, parsnips, turnips, peas. You can also add apples!)
-Small handful of red lentils and/or rice, rinsed and drained
-1 400g tin of tomatoes
-1 tbsp of oil
-1 litre of stock, any will work
-1 heaped tbsp of curry powder
-1 heaped tbsp of mango chutney
-1 heaped tbsp of tamarind paste
-Salt and pepper to taste

METHOD:

-Fry your onions, garlic, and carrots/leeks/celery in oil until they start to turn soft. You can add a touch of salt to speed this up. Add extra spices if using.
-Add in meat if using and stir until browned.
-Add in stock, tomatoes, curry powder, and tamarind.
-Add in vegetables if using, add rinsed and drained rice and/or dal. Stir through and bring soup to a boil then lower the heat. Add in chutney. Stir through.
-Keep simmering for 30 minutes, until everything is cooked through.
-Add salt and pepper to taste, feel free to be generous with the pepper.
-Serve with freshly chopped coriander, or spring onion as garnish if you wish. Serve by itself as it is very hearty, or with a side of bread, toast and chapatis work equally well.
-Enjoy!

Spanish style meatball and bean stew

I think this is one of my favourite 'necessity is the mother of invention' recipes, as it is an incredibly cheap, easy, hearty, healthy, and tasty version of traditional rustic Spanish stews (which tend to have the above qualities) that can be made from only a few ingredients that can be found in cans, and frozen meat/veg.

For a vegetarian/vegan version any meat substitute sausage/meatball would work, or you can add another tin of kidney or cannellini beans. Puy lentils also make an excellent addition to this dish.
The stew also keeps well for a few days, can be frozen, and can also be used as a pasta sauce on the reheat. You can also season this with chilli, oregano, thyme, rosemary, and bay leaves for a lighter, less smoky, and more Italian flavour if that is your preference.

INGREDIENTS:

-12 Meatballs or vegetarian/vegan equivalent
-2 400g tins of tomatoes
-1 tin of cannellini beans
-1 large red bell pepper, finely chopped
-2 onions, finely chopped
-2 carrots, finely chopped
-1 handful of spinach
-300 ml of veg/chicken/beef stock or added salt and water
-1/2 a garlic bulb, cloves crushed and chopped
-3 tsps of paprika
-1 litre of stock, any will work
-Salt to taste

METHOD:

-Fry your meatballs on a medium heat until seared and mostly cooked through. Take out and put to the side.
-Add your onion, pepper, and carrots and cook until softened. Add your garlic and stir for a few minutes without letting the garlic burn. Add paprika and other spices if using, stir for a minute.
-Add in stock/water with salt if using, and tomatoes. Add your meatballs back in. Drain and rinse your beans then add these in.
-Add your spinach and keep stirring. You could also substitute this with kale. Check your seasoning. Serve when everything is cooked through and to your desired consistency.
-Garnish with parmesan, parsley, and pepper if desired.
-Enjoy!

Chutneys, Pickles, and Sauces

Green Chutney

I love to make a spicy green chutney made from mint, coriander and chilli. Delicious as a condiment with curry and breads, it adds an extra level of freshness and spice. I also love this in most sandwiches. You can keep it in the fridge for over a week, and it freezes well in an ice cube tray.

INGREDIENTS:

-A handful of coriander, leaves and stems
-A handful of mint, leaves only
-2 to 4 chillies, depending on taste
-2 to 3 cloves of garlic, depending on taste
-1/2 an inch of ginger
-1 heaped tsp of salt
-1 heaped tsp of cumin

Optional: 1 heaped tsp of amchur (dried unripe mango), or tamarind paste, or lemon juice, to taste.

METHOD:

Whack it in a food processor and call it a day. Or if you don't have one, go old school with a mortar and pestle. It helps to grate the ginger and garlic first, and chop the herbs very finely to the extent they are almost mush. Put all the ingredients and spices together and grind with abandon. Add a touch of water if needed, but it should have a paste-like consistency.

Tomato Chutney

This is another versatile accompaniment that is in a South Indian style and often served at breakfast with idli and dosas. I tend to have this on the side with dosas, curries, pakoras, samosas, as a relish for burgers, with kebabs, on a grilled cheese naan, on the side of cheese and pickles, and my favourite is in a goat's cheese sandwich with red onion. I haven't met a dish it didn't get on with so far. It keeps in the fridge for up to a week, and freezes well.

INGREDIENTS:

-1 finely chopped onion, white or red

-1 400g tin of tomatoes

-1 tbsp of split channa (chickpea), split toor (pigeon pea), split red lentil (masoor), or peanuts if you prefer

-2 to 4 green chillies to taste, or red chilli powder (at least 1 tsp)

-3 to 4 cloves of garlic, crushed and chopped finely

-1/2 an inch of grated ginger

(Alternatively, 2 heaped tsps of ginger garlic paste would work if you don't have fresh garlic or ginger)

-1 tsp of cumin seeds or ground cumin

-Salt to taste

Optional but recommended: A touch of something acidic to help it keep for longer and add a slightly tangy flavour. You could use lemon juice to taste, or a splash of white vinegar (cider vinegar would also work) or a bit of tamarind paste with or without amchur (dried mango). You can also temper some mustard seeds with the onion, about half a tsp. You can also add a sprig of curry leaves with the onion, and garnish with chopped coriander at the end.

METHOD:

-Add a little oil to a pot on a medium heat, add in your dal and/or peanuts and stir until they go a golden colour.

-Add in your whole spices, such as mustard seed and chilli and stir until the aromas are fully released.

-Add in ginger garlic and stir for 30 seconds. Add onion, and cook until very soft. Add powdered spices. Add tomatoes, stir thoroughly and keep cooking until the smell of the raw onion and tomato dissipates.
-When the tomatoes have broken down to a thick paste, add in tamarind/vinegar/lemon juice/salt to taste.
-Take out of the pot and mix in a blender. If you don't have a blender, that's fine, just chop everything finely and don't add the dal, or use a mortar and pestle on the dal separately then with the tomato mixture.
-Enjoy!

Tamarind Chutney

You can buy tamarind concentrate and tamarind paste from most supermarkets and online, as well as your local Asian food shop. These also work perfectly well on their own in small amounts to add a burst of flavour onto most dishes and snacks. If you want to make your own tamarind chutney, here is a simple way of doing it.

INGREDIENTS:

-2 heaped tbsps of tamarind concentrate
-1 mug of boiling water
-2 tsps of sugar, ideally brown
- 1 tsp of salt
-1 tsp of ground cumin
-1 tsp of garam masala

METHOD:

-Place everything in a small pot on medium-high heat, and stir continuously for ten minutes until the mixture starts to thicken, when you get your desired consistency, allow to cool slightly then empty into a plastic or glass sealed container (like a jam jar). Green chutney and tamarind chutney are often used together as a topping for snack foods and salads, often with with yoghurt and pomegranate seeds for a burst of flavour.
-Enjoy!

Raita

Raita is an excellent accompaniment to any and all Indian dishes, and also goes particularly well with kebabs. The yoghurt and cucumber have an incredibly cooling effect on the spices found in Indian food, and the touch of spice makes it a little tangy. You can use as many or as little of the ingredients below as you wish in the raita, some people prefer it plainer and you may not have all of the ingredients listed. That is fine. This is a good alternative instead of only using plain yoghurt as a side with curries, so is also a nice treat if you are entertaining, or want to spruce up your meals a little. Make this from freshly opened yoghurt and it will last for three days. I often make this either in the yoghurt pot itself, or make it then use the yoghurt pot as easy storage for the raita.

INGREDIENTS:

-500g plain yoghurt, full or low fat
-1/2 a cucumber, chopped into very small cubes
-1 red onion, chopped very finely
-A few mint leaves, finely chopped
-A few coriander leaves, finely chopped
-1 tsp of garam masala, to taste
-1 tsp of ground cumin, to taste
-1 tsp of salt

METHOD:

-Chop all of your vegetables.
-Add this into the yoghurt.
-Add in your spices and salt.
-Stir thoroughly.
-Enjoy!

Spicy Onions

This is a recipe for the spicy, sweet, and tangy onions you often find in Indian restaurants served as a starter with papadum, or as a side dish. This recipe also happens to be incredibly easy, and one of my favourites treats!

INGREDIENTS:

-1 thinly sliced onion
-1 tsp of chilli powder
-1 tsp of salt
-5 tbsps of tomato ketchup
-2 tbsps of mango chutney
-1 tbsp of mint sauce, or dried mint
-A squeeze of lemon juice, or a dash of white wine vinegar/cider vinegar

METHOD:

-Thinly slice your onion.
-Mix all of the other ingredients together.
-Add in onion and stir thoroughly.
-Adjust salt and spice levels as necessary.
-Enjoy!

Snacks and Starters

A selection of meat, vegetarian, and vegan starters and snacks.

Chai: A proper cup of desi chai

Chai is the lifeforce on which most of South Asia, the diaspora, and beyond runs upon.

As a side note, this is chai. It is not 'chai tea', it is chai. This isn't a 'so good they named it twice scenario'. It's just chai. Chai is tea.

Here is a list of the kitchen equipment and minimum ingredients you need, and a couple of suggestions to jazz it up to your liking.

KITCHEN EQUIPMENT:

-Pot
-Sieve/tea strainer
-Mugs

BASIC INGREDIENTS:

-Loose tea leaves (you can also technically do the following with teabags)
-Cardamom pods
-Sugar
-Milk

OTHER INGREDIENTS THAT CAN BE ADDED:
-Chai Masala
-Ginger (can be powdered)
-Cinnamon
-Cloves

METHOD:
-Pour a mug of water into a pot on medium to high heat, add in loose tea leaves (one and a half tsps of tea per cup) or teabags.
-Smash a few cardamom pods and add the pods and seeds to the pot, preferably at least two per cup of tea being made.
-Add 1 1/2 tsp of sugar per cup of tea being made.
-If available: add 1 tsp of chai masala, 1/2 an inch of grated ginger, 1 stick of cinnamon, 1 or 2 cloves per cup. If using powdered spices start with half a tsp. Bring to the boil and remove from heat.
-Add milk, return to the heat, and wait until this boils. I use a mug to measure the milk, ie one mug of milk per cup, that way you get enough for how many servings you want/need plus a bit extra.
-This will take a while, as in you will start to doubt yourself and question everything. But whatever you do, keep an eye on the pot. The second you look away it will all fall apart and boil over on your hob and your house will smell like burnt sugar and/or cinnamon. Eventually, the ingredients will boil and foam will rise to the top of the pot. Either stir this foam in with a spoon, or move the pot off the heat and shake the pot gently in small circles.
-Do this three or four times at least until you have a deep, rich golden colour of the chai mixture. Finally pour through a sieve or tea strainer into a teapot, or individual mugs.
-Enjoy!

Kebabs

Treat yourself with a kebab. Super easy to make, incredibly versatile and freeze well (if there are any left!). These were Papa Singh's favourite dish in the world, and I always associate them with Christmas at my grandparents' house. They were by far the most popular thing on the menu. My Papa's recipe was very simple, he would use powdered spices, mostly chilli powder and garam masala, and finely chopped onion and chillies as that was what was readily available most of the time. Over the years I have jazzed it up a little bit with fresh ginger and garlic, but either works well, you could also add finely chopped fresh coriander. You can have these on their own as a snack, serve with rice and a little bit of yoghurt and chutney if you have it, put them in a wrap or pitta with or without your chosen sauce, or as a side dish. I have also made bigger versions of these kebabs and had them as burgers with mint sauce, which is a great alternative at barbeques. My husband likes to have them in a sandwich with a fried egg, which is also delicious, so this is the epitome of 'you do you'.

INGREDIENTS:

-500g of mince (any kind will work whether vegan mince, chicken, lamb or beef. Personally, lamb is my favourite)
-1 very finely chopped onion (any kind will work, personally I love red as it adds a bit of colour)
-2 to 4 finely chopped chillies, depending on taste
-A palm of salt (that's how Papa measured salt for this, I guess it would be about three tsps but there's something I find really satisfying about using this method as it is a wonderful memory I have of him)
-1 heaped tsp of ground cumin
-1 heaped tsp of ground coriander
-1 heaped tsp of garam masala
-1 heaped tsp of chilli powder

Optional: 3 crushed and finely chopped garlic cloves, heaped tsp of grated ginger, small bunch of finely chopped coriander.

METHOD:

-Put your mince in a large bowl, pour everything you are using on top, and mix well. If the mix isn't binding together you can add a little flour, personally I find the fat from the meat works most of the time (you can do this with a spoon but it is better to use your hands. Just wash them before and after!).
-Once everything is thoroughly mixed, shape your kebabs (if you have skewers you can do long and thin shapes, I prefer to roll small balls then flatten them a bit to make patties as that's what I was raised on).
-Put them in the oven on a baking tray at 180C or Gas Mark 4 until brown on top and cooked through, about 20-40 minutes but this will depend on the size and shape of your kebabs. You can also fry them, but I find the consistency is better when made in the oven.
-Enjoy!

Vegan Kebabs

Nutritious and delicious.

You could also add spinach, chickpeas and most other vegetables and/or cooked lentils to this dish as long as they are chopped finely, can be mashed, and are cooked with the onions and spices. If using dry lentils, cook them first in water with spices and salt, then drain and add to the veg mixture. Tinned chickpeas or other beans/lentils would be ideal as you can wash and drain then add straight to the veg mixture. I often use what I have in the cupboards and freezer, and this is a good recipe for exactly that. Cauliflower, particularly when grated, also mashes really well which is the key to this recipe. Substituting the potato for sweet potato would also work. If using frozen vegetables, I defrost them first in a freezer bag in the fridge overnight so that I can chop and grate them into smaller pieces. If you have a food processor you can cook bigger pieces often found in frozen bags of vegetables then blend, or pre-chop and freeze your own vegetables in smaller pieces for this recipe, or use fresh vegetables. If using fresh spinach add it later than the other vegetables, if using frozen add it in at the same time as everything else. You can use a heaped tbsp of ginger/garlic paste if you don't have it fresh. Keeps for 3-4 days in the fridge. These don't freeze particularly well as vegetables have a high water content and on freezing, the ice crystals break down the cell walls which affects the consistency.

These can be served with rice and/or yoghurt and chutneys as a main meal, or eaten as a snack, side dish or appetiser.

INGREDIENTS:

-4 large potatoes, skins removed, boiled, and mashed
-4 onions either brown or red, I used a mix of the two, chopped finely
-A few handfuls of peas
-A few handfuls of carrots, chopped small or grated
-10 small cauliflower florets, equivalent to a whole cauliflower, chopped small or preferably grated
-Three heaped tbsps of flour, preferably gram/chickpea (which is gluten free) but any will do. Toast your flour for a few seconds in a pan on a low heat
-1 heaped tsp ground cumin
-1 heaped tsp ground coriander
-1 heaped tsp garam masala
-1 heaped tsp chilli powder, to taste
-1 heaped tsp turmeric
-5 cloves of garlic, crushed and chopped finely
-1 inch of ginger, grated
-A palm of salt (about three tsps)
-2 to 4 chillies, depending on taste, chopped finely

Optional: Most other veg including cabbage, spinach and lentils/beans, for example tinned chickpeas. You can also add mint leaves and freshly chopped coriander if you have them

METHOD:

-Toast the flour. Do this by putting the pan on a low to medium heat, putting the flour in the pan and stirring constantly for a minute or two. You can tell when this is done as the aroma of the flour will be released and there will be a slight colour change to a subtle yellow. Be careful not to burn the flour, you just want to gently heat it. It is not advisable to eat raw flour as it can make you ill, and on top of this, the flavour isn't very nice. You can use any flour for this recipe, but gram works best.

-Boil and mash your potatoes, add salt and add half a tsp of the spices above if you want more heat and flavour, and put them to the side.

-Fry onions, and whole spices if you are using them, in a little bit of oil for a minute. Add the ginger, garlic and chillies, and cook for a minute. Add the salt and ground spices and cook for a further minute. Add the finely chopped or grated vegetables.

-You want to keep the vegetables cooking until they are soft and the moisture has evaporated. Keep stirring until the mixture is soft and dry. If it sticks to the pan, add a little water and stir thoroughly. This will take some time. When cooked, add the chopped coriander and/or mint leaves if using.

-When the vegetables are done, let them cool then mash them as much as possible, either with a food processor, potato masher, mortar and pestle, or fork.

-Add this to the mashed potatoes, add the flour, and stir together until the consistency is dough-like. If it is too wet, you can add more toasted flour or breadcrumbs. Let this cool.

-Shape your kebabs, either on a skewer so that they are long and thin, or make small round balls and press down lightly so that they are like patties.

-You can fry these, but the texture is a little prone to breaking up. I would recommend baking. Preheat the oven to 180C, lightly grease a baking tray with some oil, place the kebabs on the tray and lightly brush a little oil on top of the kebabs. Cook for a total of around 20-40 minutes, depending on the size of your kebabs, making sure to flip them over halfway through.

-Enjoy!

Grilled Cheese Naan

This is a delicious lunch/dinner/snack (and one of my favourite concoctions) that can be made from some bits and pieces. I use a mix of mango chutney and the green chutney recipe in this book, along with cheddar, cumin, and chilli. Fresh coriander would also work instead of the green chutney.
As a side note, I usually have Indian chutneys with cheese on toast or grilled cheese sandwiches and would highly recommend this.

INGREDIENTS:

-2 pack of naan
-3 tsps of mango chutney
-3 tsps of green chutney
-Cheese, grated, however much you want!
-1 red onion
-1/2 a tsp of cumin seeds, or cumin powder
-Fresh chilli or chilli flakes, to taste

METHOD:

-Grab a two pack of garlic naan (easy to find, easy to freeze, keep for ages).
-Mix up cheddar cheese, one finely chopped red onion, chopped green chilli to taste (one or two, chilli flakes would also work), 1/2 tsp of cumin seeds (preferably, though powder would work) and a small bunch of chopped fresh coriander if using.
-On one naan put a thin layer of mango chutney, and green chutney if you have it (I imagine most Indian chutneys would also work in combination but mango is the key). Spread so that there is a thin layer, you may need more or less depending on the size of your naan.
-Spread your cheese/chilli/cumin/onion combination on top.
-You could toast this under the grill as is for a sort of pizza/flatbread/open sandwich.
-Or put the other naan on top and fry in a bit of butter at medium heat for a few minutes on each side, making sure to press the sandwich down with something heavy like a pan or mortar.
-Devour!

Aloo Saag Pakora

As well as being a delicious and popular favourite, this pakora recipe is also vegan and gluten-free. This is because the gram flour, also known as besan or chickpea flour, is naturally gluten-free. You can also freeze these on the day of cooking, then allow to defrost in the fridge and heat up in the oven when you want! I like to have these with a cup of tea and ketchup. You can also make your own neon pink pakora sauce from mixing ketchup, yoghurt/mayonnaise, mint sauce, salt, and chilli powder to taste. Or have these with chutneys and pickles.

INGREDIENTS:

-2 cups besan (gram flour, also known as chickpea flour or besan)
-1 cup of water
-2 tsps of cumin seeds, or ground cumin
-1 tsp of chilli powder
-2 tsps of ground coriander
-3 tsps of salt
-500g potatoes, skinned and cubed
-Two large white or red onions, chopped
-Oil, enough for deep frying
-Handful of spinach (optional)
-2 green chillies, chopped (optional)
-Fresh coriander, chopped (optional)

METHOD:

-Mix all of the dry ingredients together (flour, spices, salt).
-Add a cup of water to this slowly while stirring the flour mixture so that you get a thick yet silky batter.
-Prepare your potatoes, you can parboil them first, or parboil then mash, but the easiest thing to do is just skin and chop them into very small pieces so that they cook when frying, they need to be the same size as finely chopped onion. Chop your onion, and add to the potato. If using frozen spinach, defrost this in the microwave first, squeeze out the excess moisture, and add. You can use coriander from frozen. Mix all of this together.
-Add your vegetables to the batter and mix.
-Heat up a lot of oil in a deep pan, you want enough that it can cover your pakora when frying. You want this to be really hot so that it sizzles when adding your mixture, but not smoking.
-Add your vegetables in batter one tbsp at a time, a good technique is to use two spoons. One to take out a measure of the vegetables in batter, and the other to roll it into the oil.
-Fry until a deep golden colour. Taste test and adjust your cooking time or oil temperature if needed.
-Enjoy!

Samosas

I don’t think there is a better combination than samosas and a cup of chai.

INGREDIENTS:

For the pastry:
-125g plain flour
-4 tbsps of oil or ghee
-5 to 6 tbsps of hot boiled water
-Cumin seeds (optional)
-Oil for frying

For the filling:
-2 small to medium-sized potatoes
-1 finely chopped red onion
-50g of peas, fresh or frozen
-1 tsp of turmeric
-1 tsp of ground cumin
-1 tsp of garam masala
-2 tsps of salt
-1 heaped tsp of ginger garlic paste, or fresh equivalent
-1 tsp of chilli powder (optional)
-1 tsp of mustard seeds (optional)
-2 tsps of amchur, or chaat masala (dried unripe ground mango, or snack food spice mix known as chaat masala, optional)

METHOD:

-Peel and chop your potatoes finely, then add into boiling water until nearly cooked, throw in your peas to cook for the last few minutes. Drain and put aside.

-In a pan, heat any whole spices you are using until the aromas are released but before the spices start to burn, then add in your onions, ginger, and garlic. Stir for a minute.

-Add in your ground spices, stir for a minute then pour in the potatoes and peas. Stir while mashing, then put aside to make the pastry.

-Mix your flour and salt into a large bowl.

-Add in the oil and mix in a circular motion mix with your fingers until it is the consistency of breadcrumbs.

-Add in the water gradually while mixing until a ball of dough forms.

-Pour out on to a surface dusted with flour and knead for a few minutes.

-Roll out your dough. Try to get this as thin as possible while still able to hold the filling in before cutting into triangles.

-Using a bit of water, rub two of the edges of the triangles until they start to form a slight paste on top. Use these two sides and press them together so you get a cone shape.

-Take your filling and place this inside, pushing down without breaking the cone apart. With a little bit of water on your finger, wet the edges of the remaining side of pastry, then press this together so that it forms a triangle. Repeat until you have no filling and/or pastry left.

-In a deep pan pour at least two inches of oil and heat until hot but not smoking. Place your samosa in the oil carefully using a spoon or tongs. Fry for 6 to 7 minutes, turning halfway through or until golden on both sides. Try the first one to make sure your oil temperature and timings are correct. Fry the rest of the samosas, and enjoy!

Aloo Chaat

This is a quick snack to be eaten on the spot. I usually make this after a spice run to my local Asian food shop when I am chopping herbs to freeze for use at a later date, and am also too hungry to wait for a curry to be finished. It's a spicy, tangy, salty and extremely tasty fried potato dish that is quick and easy to whip up. This recipe uses tamarind paste and chaat masala mix both of which can be found online and at your local Asian food shop. This is based on a popular Indian street food that is one of my favourites, and this recipe makes 3 to 4 servings. If you don't have fresh mint or coriander, or mint chutney, the green chutney in this book is an excellent substitute, just stir it in with the salt and spices or put a few tsps on top along with tamarind paste and yoghurt. The amount of sauces you put on top will be up to you, personally I love quite a bit of all to get the full mix of flavours.

INGREDIENTS:

-3/4 potatoes, cubed

-2 finely chopped red onions

-2 finely chopped green chillies

-2 tsps of salt, preferably pink salt

-3 tsps of chaat spice mix, to taste (or amchur)

-1 inch of grated ginger

-Handful of finely chopped coriander

-A few mint leaves, finely chopped

-Tamarind sauce

-Mint/green chutney

-Yoghurt

METHOD:

-Fry or bake your potato cubes.
-When finished, dry off excess oil if fried, then mix with salt and chaat mix. You can also use amchur (dried and ground unripe mango).
-Mix up the ginger, green chilli, mint, coriander and red onion in a bowl then add this to the potatoes, stir well.
-Put into a bowl to serve and add a dollop of yoghurt, 1 tsp of mint/green chutney, a squirt of tamarind sauce, and a pinch of chilli powder if desired.
-Enjoy!

Malaysian Satay

These satay sticks are just ideal for a barbeque. If you don't have one, simply put them under the grill or in the oven on the highest heat setting. Based on a popular street food in Malaysia.

INGREDIENTS:

-500g of steak, chicken, lamb, or pork. If using chicken, thigh meat is much better than breast
-2 tsps of soy sauce
-1 tsp of honey
-1 tsp of chilli powder, less if you don't like your food too spicy
-1 tsp of ground cumin
-2 tbsps of oil
-1 tsp of any curry powder

METHOD:

-Simply mix all the ingredients together to make a marinade.
-Cube up your meat and place in the marinade. Leave overnight.
-Use either bamboo or steel kebab sticks to skewer your pieces of meat.
-Grill on the barbeque or under a very hot grill until cooked through and slightly charred.

OPTIONAL SAUCE:

If you want to dip your satays into a tasty accompaniment, simply fry a finely chopped onion with two cloves of garlic until the onion turns golden brown. Then add half a tsp of chilli powder, two tsps of curry powder, an inch of grated ginger, a dash of vinegar, and half a tub of crunchy peanut butter, a tsp of salt, and a cup of water. Stir thoroughly and simmer until the mixture thickens.

Chana Aloo Chaat

Chana Aloo Chaat is made from chickpeas and potatoes, but you can use this recipe on pretty much any vegetable or fruit mix, I sometimes just use tinned chickpeas by themselves. It has a tangy, zesty, spicy, sweet and sour flavour. Also note that the amchur and tamarind are the key to the flavour but can be swapped out for lime or lemon juice and/or mango chutney if you cannot find any. There are many different types of chaat, this just happens to be how I like it, so feel free to substitute or remove anything or just play around with the ingredients or amounts until you get your desired flavour. Chaat masala spice mix is also readily available and can just be used by itself or in addition to the spices below. This can be eaten hot or cold, as a snack or side dish, and my absolute favourite way is to have it in hollow puris with tamarind water and green chutney water, which is known as pani puri or golgappa. I also sometimes have the chaat and puris topped with yoghurt, pomegranate seeds, tamarind chutney, green chutney, and sev (crispy spicy noodles made from chickpea flour, you can also use Bombay Mix), which is known as dahi puri. There is a picture of dahi puri after the tamarind chutney recipe. You can also have the chaat itself with yoghurt, pomegranate seeds, chutney, and tamarind sauce on top for an explosion of flavour.

INGREDIENTS:

-1 tin of chickpeas
-2 potatoes, peeled and chopped so the cubes are about the same size as the chickpeas
-1 or 2 red onions depending on taste, or shallots, or spring onion, chopped finely
-1 to 2 green chillies, chopped finely, to taste
-1 inch of grated ginger
-1 to 2 heaped tsps of salt, preferably pink salt, to taste
-1 tbsp of tamarind paste, but brands vary in strength so do this a bit at a time to taste
-2 heaped tsps of amchur (ground dried unripe mango)
-1 tsp of garam masala
-1 tsp of ground cumin
-A sprinkle of dried mint, or a few fresh mint leaves chopped finely
-A handful of fresh coriander, leaves chopped finely

Optional but recommended: Topped with yoghurt, green chutney, tamarind chutney, pomegranate seeds, and sev. And/or stuffed in hollow puris with green chutney water and tamarind water

METHOD:

-Boil potatoes and chickpeas until cooked through, but still have a little bit of texture.
-Mix together with onion, spices, tamarind paste and/or chutney if using, chilli, and fresh mint and coriander leaves.
-Enjoy!

Bread Omelette

Here is a quick and easy brunch I like to make when I am pre-chopping and freezing ingredients for use later. My husband and I also have this most weekends. Based on a popular Indian street food dish and breakfast.

INGREDIENTS (for two servings):
-2 slices of toast
-1 red onion
-1 red pepper
-4 green chillies
-4 eggs

METHOD:
-Chop all the ingredients you need to use.
-Whisk two eggs, making sure to get as much air in as possible, so the eggs look bubbly. The goal is to make a very light and fluffy omelette.
-Shove in half the chopped ingredients for one omelette and whisk a bit more.
-Pour into a pan on medium heat.
-When the omelette is nearly cooked, wrap it around a slice of toast, or serve on top. If it falls apart that's fine! You'll just have tasty scrambled egg on toast. Repeat for second omelette.
-Enjoy!

Nargis Kebab (The Indian Scotch Egg)

Now, first of all, the Scotch egg doesn't have anything to do with Scotland. It is called as such because the process of wrapping meat around the egg is known as 'scotching'. And Scotch eggs are not British either, the British having taken the inspiration from the Mughal dish known as the Nargis kebab which is named after the Narcissus flower that they resemble when cut open. Traditionally this would have been served in a sauce, but now you find them more commonly on their own as a snack.

I use a modified version of my kebab recipe for this, and again you can use any type of mince for the Nargis kebab. For a vegetarian version, you can also simply boil and mash a few potatoes, mix in the spices below, then use the potato mixture to wrap around the eggs. You can easily buy breadcrumbs in most shops, if you can't find any, simply toast a few slices of some fresh bread until they are crispy, tear them into pieces, put the pieces on a baking tray then bake at 150C/Gas Mark 2 for twenty minutes until very dry, then put the pieces in a freezer bag and crush with a rolling pin. And there you go, fresh breadcrumbs!

These kebabs are delicious, very fun to make, keep for three days in the fridge, and are an excellent snack to make in advance and take on a picnic.

INGREDIENTS:

-500g of mince or mashed potatoes
-6 eggs
-100g of breadcrumbs
-3 tsps of salt
-3 tsps of ginger garlic paste, or equivalent fresh ginger and garlic
-1 heaped tsp of ground cumin
-1 heaped tsp of garam masala
-1 heaped tsp of ground coriander
-1 heaped tsp of red chilli powder, less if you don't like your food too spicy

METHOD:
-Bring water to a boil, then add in the eggs with shells on. Boil for five minutes, take them out, and run a cold tap over them.
-Mix up your meat or mashed potatoes with the salt and spices. Divide equally into 6 small balls.
-Deshell the eggs.
-Take a piece of cling film, or a freezer bag, and lay this out. Take a portion of the meat/potato mixture and roll this flat onto the cling film or freezer bags.
-Place an egg in the centre and use the cling film or freezer bag to gently wrap your meat/potato mixture around the egg.
-Roll this in your hands until you get an evenly shaped ball.
-Roll this in the breadcrumbs and put to the side. Repeat for every egg.
-Now, you can either deep fry for about 7 minutes each, turning halfway through, or bake at 180C/Gas Mark 4 for 15-20 minutes.
-Enjoy!

Lassi (Yoghurt smoothie)

I am very partial to a lassi on a hot day! There are many variations of lassi, my particular favorite is mango lassi, but you can also make this plain without any added fruit, or use any fresh or frozen fruit you have lying around. For a truly Indian flavour, also add a pinch of ground cardamom, or seeds from a few cardamom pods. You can also add salt, to taste, instead of sugar to make this a savoury drink.

INGREDIENTS:

-500g of plain yoghurt
-1 cup of of milk
-1 to 2 tbsps of sugar for a sweet lassi, a tsp of salt for a savoury lassi, all to taste. You will need less sugar of you are using fruit
-1/2 a tsp of ground cardamom, or seeds from three cardamom pods (if having a sweet or fruit lassi)
-A cup of mango slices, or frozen fruit

METHOD:

-Simply place everything in a blender, and blend until smooth
-Enjoy!

Vegetarian/Vegan

A selection of both vegan and vegetarian dishes.

Aloo Gobi/Mixed Vegetable Curry

This is a staple in my house. It's a simple, healthy and filling vegan curry that I always have a few portions of in the freezer at any time.

Please note there are about as many recipes for Aloo Gobi as there are grains of sand on a beach. Literally meaning 'Potato Cauliflower', and not usually the sort of thing you get on a menu, it's a cheap and cheerful traditional Punjabi home-cooked dish that every family has their own twist to, this just happens to be mine. To bulk this up, you can also add frozen or fresh veg such as spinach, peas and carrots which makes it more of a mixed vegetable curry. I often switch between Aloo Gobi by itself and adding different vegetables for a bit of variety. If you do not have fresh ginger or garlic, simply use two heaped tbsps of ginger garlic paste. Though if you can, I believe this does taste best with fresh.

When it comes to freezing the potatoes don't freeze particularly well, as they can go a bit mushy on reheating, but it does keep in the fridge for three to four days. If you are planning on freezing for later, I would slightly undercook everything then freeze without serving first, plus curry usually tastes better on the reheat anyway. Or, you can divide up portions and keep most of it to the side for freezing, then continue cooking what you need for that night. Or you can replace the potatoes with suggestions above. You can also serve, then make sure all the potatoes are eaten before freezing the rest. If you prefer a drier curry, add in the water a little at a time as you need it.

INGREDIENTS:

-4 medium/large potatoes, peeled and cut into cubes
-1 medium cauliflower cut into florets slightly larger than the potatoes

Note: These do not have to be a particular type, but I find the all-rounder potatoes and standard cauliflower are the best

-3 to 4 onions, chopped roughly
-1 400g tin of tomatoes
-1 bulb of garlic, peel, chop and crush all the cloves
-2 inches of ginger root, grated
-2 chillies, remove the stem, slice and chop (this is for a milder spice, add to taste, and I prefer to use the thin green chillies)
-2 tbsps of oil or ghee (vegetable for vegan option, ghee for vegetarian)
-3 tsps of salt, to taste
-1 heaped tsp of ground turmeric
-2 heaped tsps of ground cumin
-2 heaped tsps of ground coriander
-2 heaped tsps of garam masala

Optional: 1 tsp each of mango powder (amchur), fenugreek (methi), chilli powder, mustard seeds, 1 bay leaf. If you can, have some chopped coriander on hand, you can buy this in bulk, chop it, and freeze in portions of a small handful

METHOD:

-In a pan, heat up the oil for a minute to a medium heat.
-If you are using whole (not ground) spices, add them in now and stir until aromas are released.
-Add onion and stir until coated in the oil, keep cooking until they start to soften. If the onion starts to stick, add more oil and maybe turn the heat down a little bit.
-Add in chilli, ginger, garlic and salt and stir thoroughly.
-Add all the ground spices, coat everything. Stir for a further minute.
-Add in tinned tomatoes, stir until the smell of fresh tomatoes dissipates.
-Add in potatoes and cauliflower, stir, reduce heat after a minute. Add a cup of water.
-Let it simmer, if it starts to stick to the pan add in a bit of water at a time, and some salt. You can also add in vegetable stock, or another 400g tin of tomatoes of there really isn't enough moisture but this will make the spices less effective therefore you may need to add a bit more spice. If there is too much moisture, keep it simmering until you get the consistency you want.
-If you are adding more frozen vegetables, do this when the potato and cauliflower are half-cooked, as they will also release moisture.
-Check if the vegetables are cooked by stabbing them with a fork until you get the texture you like. If you are freezing without serving, make sure it is a little undercooked for the reheat.
-If you wish, just before serving stir in another tsp of garam masala and chopped coriander if you have it. If it is frozen, you may need to stir it in for a minute or two.

TIPS: If it tastes a little bland try adding a bit more salt and/or garam masala, if it is not spicy enough you can add in another freshly chopped chilli, if it is too spicy serve with a bit of yoghurt or have a glass of milk, if it doesn't quite have enough 'bite' you can stir in a freshly chopped red onion.

Restaurant-style Tadka Dal

This is a classic vegetarian or vegan side dish, depending on what you use to fry your ingredients, that is found on most Indian restaurant menus. 'Tadka' refers to tempering spices and onions, and this is normally done separately then added to lentils that have been cooked with a little salt and spices. I have simplified this to a 'one-pot' version, though if you wish to be a bit more traditional you can fry some whole spices in oil such as mustard seed, cumin seed, cloves, bay leaves, curry leaves, a clove or two of garlic, and chopped or whole chilli for a minute or until the aromas are released, then pour on top of the dal to really make this dish out of this world! You can also simply add some crispy onions on top. Any combination of Indian spices will suffice so use what you have available and I do encourage you to experiment. I have even used crushed cardamom pods in my tadka to add a sweet and aromatic underlying flavour to dals. Most of the time I use another onion, a tsp of cumin seeds, a tsp of mustard seeds, whole dried chillies, a tsp of ginger garlic paste, a bay leaf, and two cloves. I then heat up a tbsp of oil to a medium heat, fry the onion until crispy, throw everything else in to sizzle for a few seconds until the aromas are released, and then I pour this straight on top of the dal before serving. To freeze, simply stir in the tadka and store in resealable plastic tubs or tightly tied freezer bags. On the reheat, I add a little chilli oil, chopped coriander and chopped red onion if I have it. This is delicious by itself with rice or bread, and also makes an excellent side dish. I quite like to have a few portions of this in the freezer in smaller portions so I can heat them up as accompaniments to something else, but I also love to have a big bowl of this with a pile of rice for ultimate comfort food.

INGREDIENTS:

-2 tbsp of ginger garlic paste (or 1 garlic bulb, cloves crushed and roughly chopped, and 2 inches of grated ginger)
-1 400g tin of tomatoes, if you don't have tinned tomatoes you can just add more water and salt/vegetable stock
-1 heaped tsp of garam masala
-1 heaped tsp of turmeric
-1 heaped tsp of dried coriander
-2 heaped tsps of cumin

-2 heaped tsps of salt
-2 chillies and/or 1 tsp of chilli powder, and/or curry powder, to taste
-2 to 3 onions (depending on method)
-1 cup of split chickpea (chana), or split pigeon pea (toor/arhar) also known as split red gram, or split red lentil (masoor). Feel free to combine any of the above as well! I use 1/3 split chana, 1/3 toor and 1/3 masoor as I often have them lying around, and I love the rich texture and colour they create when combined together
-4 cups of water

Optional: Whole spices for the tadka, chopped fresh coriander

METHOD:

-Rinse the dal several times and drain.
-Fry two onions in a big pot until translucent. Add ginger, garlic, and chilli. Stir for a minute.
-Add in ground spices and coat the onions.
-Add tomatoes, or stock if using, stir for a minute. Add lentils and coat. Add water.
-Boil this for 40 minutes on a relatively high heat, occasionally checking the consistency, spice/taste level, and making sure nothing has stuck to the bottom of the pan. (More time cooking=thicker sauce). Skim any foam that appears on top.

Optional: Fry another onion or two in oil with your choice of a few whole spices, chilli, and ginger garlic until the aromas are released and/or the onion is crispy. Then simply pour this on top of your dal, serve, and enjoy!

Super easy and quick chana saag

Here's a very simple and quick way of cooking up a can of chickpeas that I like to add frozen spinach to. You could also add peppers and/or peas. This is so easy, I often make this as a side dish while cooking rice and heating up a frozen portion of curry I made earlier which makes it a perfect midweek meal. This also tastes great in wraps, or as a cold salad!

INGREDIENTS:

-1 tin of chickpeas
-1 400g tin of tomatoes
-1 tbsp of ginger garlic paste, or equivalent fresh
-1 onion
-1 tsp of mustard seeds
-2 crushed cardamom pods
-2 cloves
-1 bay leaf
-1 heaped tsp of ground coriander
-1 heaped tsp of ground cumin
-2 heaped tsps of garam masala
-One heaped tsp of turmeric
-Salt, to taste
-Dried chillies, to taste

METHOD:

-Temper any whole seeds in pot with oil on a medium heat until the aromas are released. You only want to use 1 tsp of mustard seeds, 2 cloves, 1 bay leaf, and 2 cardamom pods per tin of chickpeas, with chilli to taste.
-Add a finely chopped onion and fry for a minute or two. Stir well.
-Add ginger and garlic, and fry for another minute or two.
-Add in your ground spices and stir well. Reduce the heat a bit.
-Add tinned tomatoes and cook until the smell of tomatoes dissipates.
-Drain and rinse your tinned chickpeas, add to the pot with frozen spinach. -Stir regularly until cooked through. Add salt to taste.
-Enjoy!

Dal Makhani

Most of the recipes I have included here are very easy, this dish is a bit more of a labour of love but it is so worth it. This isn't usually an everyday type of dal as it is quite rich, but you will find it at most restaurants and any wedding or family function, as it is incredibly delicious and therefore extremely popular but a bit more effort than the usual fare. After experimenting over the years, I believe this is the easiest way to get that proper restaurant taste. The key to a Punjabi Dal Makhani is a hearty, creamy, thick and buttery texture, with an aromatic and sweet warmth without being too spicy. Soaking your whole lentils overnight or for at least 4-6 hours in the morning before cooking is absolutely needed to get that texture. Using whole spices such as cinnamon bark, cloves, and cardamom pods also really help this recipe. For a proper traditional taste you ideally want to cook this with butter/ghee then add cream, but a vegetarian/vegan version using oil and coconut milk also works brilliantly. Use coconut milk for freezing portions so that it doesn't separate on the reheat. This is a great recipe for a slow cooker (just put everything in and cook on high for 8 hours or low for 12) or pressure cooker (fry your onions and spices, then add in lentils, tomatoes, and water then cook for 40 minutes). In all versions, add your cream or coconut milk right at the end so that it doesn't separate at a higher heat. This recipe is for one cup of whole urid dal (black gram) and half a cup of mixed kidney beans (rajma) and half a cup of black eyed beans (lobia) so just scale up if you want to make more. The black-eyed peass are optional but I think they add to the creamy texture of the dal.

INGREDIENTS:

-1 cup of whole black gram
-1/2 a cup of kidney beans
(Optional: 1/2 a cup of dried black-eyed peass)
-2 tbsps of butter, ghee or oil (at least!)
-3 cardamom pods, crush and use seeds (or 1/2 tsp to 1 tsp of ground cardamom)
-2 cloves
-1 bay leaf
-1 to 2 inch cinnamon stick (or one tsp of cinnamon powder)
-2 heaped tsps of cumin seeds or ground cumin
-1 heaped tsp of turmeric
-2 heaped tsps of ground coriander
-1 heaped tsp of garam masala
-1 tsp of chilli powder or 1 to 2 green chillies, to taste
-3 heaped tsps of salt
-3 heaped tsps of crushed garlic
-2 heaped tsps of crushed ginger
-2 onions
-2 400g tins of tomatoes
-4 cups of water (more or less)
-1 tin of coconut milk or cream to taste

Optional: Chopped coriander and more cream to garnish

METHOD:

-Soak your dry whole lentils in a covered pot overnight, or at least 4-6 hours. Rinse and drain. If you are using canned kidney beans, you do not need to soak them.
-Apply a generous amount of oil/ghee/butter to the pan on a medium high heat.
-Add whole spices to the pan and stir through until the aromas are released, so 30 seconds maximum, but do not burn the spices. Add your ginger and garlic and fry for a few seconds.
-Add your onions and ground spices, cook for a minute or two, then lower the heat slightly. Add more oil if the pan is dry. You want to soften the onions as much as possible without going crispy.
-Add in your lentils, stir until coated.
-Add in your chopped tomatoes, and water so that the lentils are covered and fully submerged.
-Bring to the boil, then lower the heat and simmer for at least an hour and a half to two hours, checking the consistency of the lentils regularly. If the mixture begins to stick to the bottom of the pan, try to lower the heat or add more water and a touch more salt.
-When the lentils have become very soft and the dal is thick, slowly stir in your cream or milk to taste. Remove whole spices such as the cinnamon and bay leaves before serving.
-Garnish with freshly chopped coriander and a touch more cream or coconut milk.
-Enjoy!

Palak Paneer

Paneer is a really tasty cottage cheese that is used in a lot of Indian vegetarian dishes, and for a vegan version you can substitute tofu. Palak paneer is extremely popular, delicious, vegetarian, gluten free, and high in protein, calcium, iron, as well as low fat (without cream), and can be made in under 30 minutes. You can make this from frozen spinach and paneer. If using frozen paneer for this recipe, defrost it first by putting the paneer in a freezer bag then in a bowl of hot boiled water, but not so hot that the paneer starts to cook. Then for fresh or from frozen paneer you can either fry the cubes first in a little oil for two minutes while turning halfway until they turn a bit golden, then soak them in hot boiled water, or if you don't want to fry them just soak the cubes in hot boiled water for 10 to 20 minutes, while cooking everything else and add in towards the end of the cooking process. This will keep the texture of the paneer creamy and stop it drying out and/or turning rubbery. If using frozen spinach, defrost this first in the microwave for before use and then run it under a cold tap then squeeze out the extra moisture. If using fresh spinach, to keep the colour and a pleasant consistency you will need to put your leaves in a colander, pour over boiling water, then cold water, drain and cool, and squeeze out the extra moisture. Some people like to blitz the onion and ginger garlic together, or the spinach with a mug of water and/or cashew nuts for a creamier texture, and you could also do both but do not do these together as onion and spinach cook at different times. You can also add a touch of cream or coconut milk at the end. Often called Saag Paneer, the difference is that Saag is a mixture of leafy greens, particularly spinach and mustard though this can also be spring greens and finely chopped broccoli, whereas Palak is the Hindi for spinach, and Palak curries are made from only spinach. The spices and method of preparation are the same.

INGREDIENTS:

-250g paneer
-250g spinach
-1 to 2 green chillies to taste, or 1/2 to 1 whole tsp of chilli powder to taste, add a bit more of you want it spicy
-1 heaped tbsp of ginger garlic paste, or at least 5 crushed and chopped cloves of garlic and an inch of grated ginger
-3 onions, white or red, finely chopped
-1 drained 400g tin of chopped tomatoes, or four medium sized fresh tomatoes finely chopped, you can also give this a miss if you want a really dry curry
-2 heaped tsps of garam masala
-1 tsp of turmeric
-1 tsp of cumin

Optional but recommended: 2 cloves, 1 tsp of methi (dried fenugreek), 2 green cardamom pod seeds, 1/2 inch of cinnamon bark or a 1/4 tsp of cinnamon, 1 tsp of mustard seed, a squeeze of lemon juice right at the end and/or freshly chopped coriander and/or red onion for garnish

METHOD:

-Prepare your paneer and greens, please see note above for more details as this is different if you are using fresh or frozen ingredients, and personal taste.
-Fry whole spices if using in a little oil until aromas are released.
-Add in onion, ginger, and garlic, or onion and ginger garlic paste, add fresh chillies if using, add a tsp of salt, fry until the onions turn golden and are significantly reduced. Add more oil or water if necessary.
-Add ground spices, cook for a minute or two. Add tomatoes and cook until they break down and turn mushy and the fresh smell of tomatoes dissipates.
-Add half a mug of water, a little more if needed to deglaze the pan, and cook until the mixture thickens, about five to six minutes, stirring regularly so the mixture doesn't stick to the bottom of the pan. You want to reduce the amount of moisture to your personal preference, so take a bit longer if you wish. Reduce heat if necessary.
-Lower the heat if you haven't already. Remove cinnamon stick. Add in spinach or spinach puree, cook for two to three minutes. Add cream or coconut milk if using. Check your seasoning and add salt if necessary.
-Drain and stir in paneer for two minutes, add in lemon juice, or cream or coconut milk if using, remove whole spices, garnish with freshly chopped coriander and/or a little chopped red onion.
-Enjoy!

Rajma Chawal

The kidney bean is not native to the Indian subcontinent, instead they were brought over from South America by the Portuguese (same with chillies and potatoes, rather surprisingly given how ubiquitous they are in South Asian cuisine). However, the beans have become a staple in a lot of South Asian cooking, particularly in the more Northern regions. This dish is known as Rajma Chawal, which translates to 'kidney beans rice', as Rajma tends to specify a very particular type of dal made in Punjab and Nepal, and is almost always served with boiled rice. This is a very easy dal, you can cook it using kidney beans from a can rather than having to soak pulses overnight, it keeps well in the freezer, and is very filling and creamy while being low in fat as the buttery texture comes from the beans themselves rather than added cream or yoghurt and kidney beans are naturally low in fat. This is one of the most popular dishes in Punjab, Nepal, Himachal Pradesh, and Jammu, as kidney beans grow well in the climate. Should you happen to be invited over to someone's house for a basic lunch this will probably feature on the menu somewhere.

INGREDIENTS:

-3 cans of kidney beans or equivalent
-2 finely chopped or grated onions
-2 400g tins of tomatoes
-1 heaped tbsp of ginger garlic paste, or fresh equivalent
-1 heaped tsp of turmeric
-2 heaped tsps of ground coriander
-1 heaped tsp of cumin
-1 heaped tsp of garam masala
-1/2 a tsp of chilli powder
-1 tbsp of oil/ghee
-2 to 3 tsps of salt, to taste
-3 to 4 cups of water

Optional but recommended: 2 bay leaves, 2 cardamom pods (use the crushed seeds), ½ inch stick of cinnamon, or ½ a tsp of cinnamon powder

METHOD:

-If using whole dry kidney beans, you will need to rinse them, then soak these in boiling water overnight (as in put the beans in a pan then pour boiling water over them and leave a tea towel on top). You will need at least twice the amount of cups of water than cups of beans. Then drain and rinse before use. Otherwise use three cans.
-Add your finely chopped onion to a pan with oil at a medium heat. After a minute add salt to help the moisture come out. Add your whole spices, careful not to burn them. You want to cook the onion for a while, until it starts to turn brown, so throw your whole spices in just before the onion changes colour. Add your ground spices. Fry for 30 seconds, making sure you don't burn them and add more oil if necessary.
-Add your ginger garlic. Fry for a further minute or two. Add tomatoes and stir thoroughly. Add your drained and rinsed beans. Add water until the beans are covered.
-Cook this to submission on a high heat, until the lentils turn very soft and the onions/tomatoes completely break down to a paste. If you want to speed things up, once the beans are fully cooked you can blend part of the mixture and then add it back in for a creamy paste. Add more water a bit at a time if it sticks to the pan.
-Remove any whole spices such as cinnamon and bay leaves. Garnish with chopped coriander, finely chopped red onion, or a touch of cream. Serve with boiled rice, preferably with a tsp of turmeric and cumin seeds in the boiling water to create a brightly coloured and aromatic accompaniment.
-Enjoy!

Mattar Paneer

A classic vegetarian paneer dish that is incredibly popular in Northern India. Simple ingredients, tasty, and easy. Can be made from frozen ingredients but defrost your paneer in a bag in hot water before use, and you can use either fresh or frozen peas but frozen peas will take a while longer to cook and add more moisture. I have also seen some people add chopped cauliflower florets to this, and I tend to be more of a pragmatist than a purist, so go ahead. You can choose to fry your paneer first for two minutes until slightly golden, turning halfway through, then remove from the pan and soak until needed, then add back in to the curry for the last minute of cooking, or just add in the paneer at the end for two minutes without frying first. I always recommend soaking your paneer in hot boiled water for at least ten minutes before cooking it in the curry as that way more moisture is retained and the paneer will be creamier, whether you choose to fry first or not. You can add a touch of cream or coconut milk to this recipe for a smooth and velvety sauce, or keep it on the lighter side like I did here. Another way to get a creamier sauce without adding anything is to blitz together the onion, chillies, and ginger garlic in a food processor to form a puree then add this after the whole spices if using, then the tomatoes, ground spices and salt, then just follow the rest of the recipe. Or you can cook the onion, chillies, and ginger garlic until the onions turn golden, then add tomatoes and cook for a minute, then put this in a food processor to form a thick gravy. You would then fry whole spices if using for under a minute, then add the gravy, add ground spices, then follow the rest of the recipe.

INGREDIENTS:

-250g of paneer
-1 tin of chopped tomatoes, of four to five freshly chopped tomatoes
-150g to 200g of peas depending on preference, fresh or frozen
-3 to 4 onions, white or red
-1 heaped tbsp of ginger garlic paste, or 5 cloves of garlic crushed and finely chopped, and 1 inch of grated ginger at least
-1 to 2 green chillies, or 1/2 a tsp to a tsp of chilli powder, more if you want it spicy
-2 heaped tsps of garam masala
-1 heaped tsp of cumin, ground or whole seeds
-1 heaped tsp of ground coriander
-1 heaped tsp of turmeric

Optional but recommended: 1 bay leaf, 1 inch of cinnamon bark or ¾ of a tsp of ground cinnamon, 1 tsp of methi (ground fenugreek), 2 cardamom pod seeds, cream or coconut milk if desired, a handful of freshly chopped coriander leaves for garnishing with

METHOD:
-Fry whole spices if using for under a minute or until the aromas are released but without burning them.
-Add onions, chillies, and ginger garlic and cock until onions soften and turn golden. Add a touch of salt to speed this up.
-Add ground spices, stir through thoroughly and cook for another minute.
-Add tomatoes, cook until mushy and the raw smell of tomatoes dissipates, so at least a minute or two. Add in half a cup to a cup of water and simmer until you get your chosen consistency.
-Add the peas and a cup of water then cook until everything thickens, adding more water if needed. Taste test and add more salt or spice if necessary.
-When the peas are cooked to your preferred level of bite, throw in your paneer for two minutes if you haven't fried it, then take the heat off. If you have fried your paneer beforehand just stir through thoroughly for a minute.
-Add cream or coconut milk if using, then finally garnish with freshly chopped coriander if you have it and serve.
-Enjoy!

Moong Dal

Slightly confusingly, in English this dal is known as 'green gram' when whole, 'green lentils' when split, and 'split/petite yellow lentils' when dehusked and split. We always had it whole, and it was always called moong. You can use split, it just means that you don't need to soak the lentils before and the cooking time will be reduced using (though you can soak them in boiling water for 15-20 minutes to further reduce the cooking time), but the flavour and texture will be significantly different and more similar to a Tarka Dal. This dal is not massively popular or well known outside home cuisine, as you don't tend to see it on menus, but it is a childhood favourite for me and very popular in the Northern regions of the Indian subcontinent as a dal, as well as across Asia as an ingredient in both sweet and savoury dishes. In South India this lentil can be used to make dosas, and in East Asia is used as a dessert ingredient and for sweet pancakes, and in South East Asia is used as part of a fish and seafood broth, as well as being used to make bean sprouts. Moong also features in some Middle Eastern dishes served with rice.

This dal recipe is very simple and spicy, as my grandparents would make this before there was the readily available abundance of spices today. Most of the flavour comes from salt, garlic, ginger, and chillies or chilli powder, as well as the dal itself. When staying with them we ate it at least twice a week, and a childhood memory is the big pressure cooker sitting on the counter in the kitchen filled to the brim with Moong dal from which dinners were decanted.

Feel free to add a bay leaf, curry leaves, lemon juice, or added ginger. I like to keep it simple as it is a comfort food for me, and I always have what I need to make it. Moong can become a bit soupy, so I add very roughly chopped onion and black-eyed peas for a bit of texture (and also that's what I am used to) but lots of people enjoy it by itself without black-eyed peas. I normally just have the lentils themselves, but when I have a few potatoes that needed using up I finely chopped them and added them to the boiling dal until everything is cooked through, you could do the same with spinach, peas, or carrots. If you are using whole lentils, soak them overnight with boiling water (put the dal in a pot, add boiling water, at least twice as many cups as the dal, and cover with a tea towel, dish, or cling film, then rinse before use). This keeps for 3 days in the fridge when cooked, and freezes very well.

INGREDIENTS:

-2 cups of whole green gram
-1 cup of black-eyed peas (optional)
-5 onions, white or red, roughly chopped or sliced
-1 400g tin of tomatoes (you can also substitute with vegetable stock, or just boiling water and added salt)
-2 heaped tbsps of ginger garlic paste, or one whole garlic, cloves crushed and finely chopped, and two inches of grated fresh ginger
-2 tsps of red chilli powder, hot curry powder, or 4 green chillies, reduce for less heat
-2 heaped tsps of ground coriander
-2 heaped tsps of ground cumin
-2 heaped tsps of turmeric
-2 heaped tsps of garam masala
-4 tsps of salt, to taste
-Oil/ghee
-6 cups of water

METHOD:

-If using whole dry pulses soak them overnight with boiling water (put the dal in a pot, add boiling water, at least twice as many cups as the dal, and cover with a tea towel, dish, or cling film). Then drain and rinse before use.
-Add whole spices into a pan with oil at a medium heat, if using whole spices, stir until the aromas are released. Add ginger garlic paste, or fresh ginger and garlic, and stir for a minute at most, add more oil if it begins to stick as you don't want to burn the garlic.
-Add onions and fry on a medium high heat until they soften, add salt to speed this up.
-Add ground spices and coat the onions, careful that the spices don't stick to the bottom of the pan and burn as that will leave an acrid taste. Add a little oil or water if this happens.
-Add tomatoes, or stock, or water and salt. Stir thoroughly.
-Add in lentils, add water so that everything is covered.

-Bring to a boil, then lower the heat slightly and cook for at least an hour, occasionally stirring and checking the consistency as well as making sure nothing is sticking to the pan. Add a little more water if necessary.
-Serve with rice and/or roti/chapati, and chutney and/or pickles if you wish. This works as a main and a side dish. Garnish with chopped coriander if you have it.
-Enjoy!

Saag Aloo

Here's a simple and quick classic vegan curry that works well as a main and side dish, and can be served with rice or roti/chapati.

INGREDIENTS:
-500g potatoes, cubed
-2 large onions, chopped
-400g of fresh or frozen spinach
-1 heaped tbsp of ginger garlic paste, or at least1 inch of freshly grated ginger and at least five cloves of garlic
-1 400g tin of tomatoes
-2 tsps of cumin seeds or ground cumin
-2 tsps of black mustard seed
-1 tsp of turmeric
-1 heaped tsp of ground coriander
-1 heaped tsp of garam masala
-1/2 to 1 tsp of chilli powder, or one to two chillies, to taste
-2 tsps of salt, to taste
-1 tbsp of oil/ghee

Optional but recommended: 1 heaped tsp of ground fenugreek (methi), 1 bay leaf, a touch of lemon juice, a handful of chopped coriander

METHOD:

-Add oil to a pan and when it reaches a medium high heat add your mustard seed and other whole spices.

-When the mustard seeds start to dance, add in your onions, stir for a minute, then add your ginger garlic and cook until the onions turn soft. Add your ground spices and stir in thoroughly, careful not to burn the spices or ginger garlic on the bottom of the pan. Add a little more oil if this happens. Cook for a further minute.

-Add in your tomatoes and salt to taste, stir thoroughly again. Add potatoes and a touch of water if needed so that they are mostly covered. When the potatoes start to soften slightly add your spinach. If you are using frozen, you will need to add less water to the potatoes as frozen vegetables release a lot of moisture.

-Keep on the heat until the potatoes are cooked through, stirring occasionally so that nothing sticks to the bottom of the pan.

-If you like, add a handful of chopped coriander and a squeeze of lemon before serving.

-Enjoy!

Chana Dal

A simple and easy classic vegan curry that is ideal for bulk cooking and freezing. This is made with split chickpeas, you can also use canned whole chickpeas just halve the water and cooking time. This is a great recipe to add coconut milk to, but freezing coconut milk can be variable so only add when serving. This is lovely by itself, with rice and/or roti/chapati, and can be a main or side dish. You can add more water if you prefer a soupier texture.

INGREDIENTS:
-2 cups of split chickpeas
-2 onions, very finely chopped
-4 cloves of garlic and 1 inch of grated ginger, or 1 tbsp of ginger garlic paste
-1 400g tin of tomatoes
-2 tbsps of salt
-2 heaped tsps of garam masala
-2 heaped tsps of cumin
-2 heaped tsps of ground coriander
-1 tsp of turmeric
-1 heaped tsp of methi (dried fenugreek, you can skip this if you don't have it)
-1 tsp of chilli powder, less if you don't want it spicy
-2 bay leaves
-4 cloves

METHOD:

-Soak your chickpeas in two cups of boiling water for 20 to 30 minutes. Drain and rinse. If using canned chickpeas skip this step.
-Fry your onions in two tbsps of oil until they turn soft.
-Add in your bay leaves and cloves, fry for a minute.
-Add in your ginger and garlic, fry for two minutes.
-Add your spices and stir thoroughly ensuring all the onions are coated.
-Add in your tomatoes, stir thoroughly.
-Add in your chickpeas and five cups of water.
-Bring to a boil then simmer for an hour or until the chickpeas are tender, checking occasionally and adding more water if needed.
-Garnish with freshly chopped coriander if you have it.
-Enjoy!

Punjabi Chole

This is an incredibly common snack food throughout Punjab, most commonly served with fried breads such as bhature and puri, or plain rice and/or chapati (I love it in wraps with rice and/or salad and a touch of yoghurt like an Indian burrito interpretation). It is similar to a chana dal or chana masala, but with a stronger and more complex flavour, and a thicker gravy. It is tangy, aromatic, and spicy with an underlying sweetness. By itself, it's quite healthy for such a hearty Punjabi dish as chickpeas are rich in protein and fibre, it is made without any added cream or butter, and vegan if you use oil instead of ghee. This dish is normally made with chole, which are a larger version of chana (chickpeas), but I have found that canned chickpeas work very well. The main ingredients are black tea, tamarind paste (a decent squeeze of lemon juice with a touch of brown sugar can be substituted), amchur (dried mango powder, though again added lemon juice can work as a substitute, as can tamarind paste), and black cardamom (though green cardamom also works well). You can also find masala mixes in most Asian food shops, and they work brilliantly. Another trick is to soak chickpeas in the black tea before cooking them, if using dried chickpeas you can do this overnight and if using chickpeas from a can do this for 30 minutes. You can leave out the cumin or cinnamon if you wish and instead substitute with a tsp of mango chutney.

INGREDIENTS:

-2 cans of chickpeas, rinsed and drained

-1 mug of black tea made with two teabags (you can use loose leaf tea if you wish and sieve out the leaves, but standard teabags work just as well)

-2 to 4 chopped green chillies, to taste

-1 to 2 onions, white or red, very finely chopped or pureed with tomato paste

-100g of tomato paste (I often add a bit more than this and less water so that the chole becomes thicker, almost like the texture of refried beans as I like to have it in wraps. You can also use a can of tomatoes or fresh tomatoes)

-1 heaped tbsp and a half of ginger garlic paste, or equivalent grated ginger and crushed and finely chopped garlic

-1 tbsp of tamarind paste, or more to taste (I often put in two as I love the flavour of tamarind)

-2 bay leaves

-3 to 4 crushed cardamom pod seeds, or three black cardamom pods for a sweeter and smokier flavour

-4 cloves

-2 heaped tsp of methi (dried fenugreek)

-2 heaped tsps of amchur (dried mango powder)

-1 heaped tsp of red chilli powder, to taste

-1 heaped tsp of cumin

-1 tsp of sugar (this is to cut the acidity of the tomatoes, you can leave it out if you feel like it doesn't need it, or add more cinnamon)

-1/2 tsp of ground cinnamon, or small stick of cinnamon

-Salt to taste

-Oil

METHOD:

-Fry any whole spices for a minute in a touch of oil on a low heat until the aromas are released.
-Add in ginger garlic, fry for a minute at a slightly higher temperature.
-Add in onion, fry for a minute.
-Add tomatoes, tea, tamarind, and ground spices.
-Add in drained chickpeas. Add water if needed so that the chickpeas are covered. Remove whole spices if you wish.
-Simmer until you get your desired consistency, about 20-40 minutes, adding salt to taste, and garnish with sliced red onion, chopped coriander, and fresh ginger, or even a bit of mint.
-Enjoy!

Sweet and creamy coconut vegan dal

Here is a quick and easy one-pot coconut vegan dal. This dish is sweet, aromatic, and filling without being too spicy.

Great by itself with rice, but also makes an excellent accompaniment to other, more fiery, dishes. You can also add potatoes, sweet potatoes and butternut squash to this dal for a really hearty vegan dinner. This particular recipe also freezes well and is ideal for cooking in bulk.

INGREDIENTS:

-2 cups of split lentils (for this dal I often use toor or split pigeon pea, but split mung also known as yellow lentils, split chana/chickpeas, or masoor also known as red lentils also work very well)
-1 400g tin of tomatoes
-1 tin of coconut milk
-3 onions chopped very finely
-2 heaped tbsp of ginger garlic paste, or a garlic with the cloves crushed and chopped and a 2 inch piece of grated ginger
-2 green chillies or 1 tsp of chilli powder
-1 large stick of cinnamon, at least 3 inches, or a tsp of cinnamon powder
-4 green cardamom pods, crush them and use the seeds, or a tsp of cardamom powder
-1 heaped tsp of turmeric
-3 heaped tsps of ground coriander
-2 heaped tsps of ground cumin
-2 heaped tsps of garam masala
-2 tbsps of oil
-5 cups of water
-Salt to taste, about 3 tsps

Optional but recommended: 2 tsps of mustard seeds

METHOD:

-Heat up oil in a pan to a medium heat, then add in whole spices and toast for thirty seconds and/or until the aromas are released.
-Add in your ginger and garlic, and stir for thirty seconds.
-Add in your chopped onion, and fresh chillies if using, and cook for two minutes until they start to turn soft.
-Add in your ground spices and stir for two minutes.
-Add in your tomatoes, stir thoroughly, and cook for two minutes until a paste starts to form and you can no longer smell the tomatoes.
-Rinse and drain your lentils, add to the pot and stir thoroughly
-Add in five cups of water and salt.
-Bring this to a boil, then lower the heat and keep it bubbling away for about forty minutes. Stir occasionally to make sure nothing is sticking to the bottom of the pan, and add more water a cup at a time if this happens. If you are adding in other vegetables, put these in halfway through the cooking time.
-When the lentils are tender and the liquid has reduced considerably, lower the heat and add in your coconut milk. Stir thoroughly.
-Simmer at a very low heat for five minutes.
-Enjoy!

Jeera Aloo

This is a classic, simple, and easy potato curry that is most commonly served as a side dish.

I often make this as a side dish while I am defrosting something else, which turns a midweek meal of leftovers in to a bit more of an exciting feast. This dish is also great by itself as a snack, or as a main dish served with rice and/or breads. You can make this easily without onion or garlic, personally I add a little red onion towards the end for added crunch and colour. If using white onion, I would add this to the pan with the whole spices and fry until it turns soft. This is vegan, very quick, and uses only a few ingredients.

INGREDIENTS:

-500g potatoes, cubed
-1 tbsp of ginger garlic paste, or fresh equivalent
-2 green chillies, chopped (less if you don't like your food too spicy)
-2 tsps of cumin seeds (if you don't have cumin seeds, just use ground cumin)
-1 heaped tsp of turmeric
-1 heaped tsp of ground cumin
-1 heaped tsp of ground coriander
-1 heaped tsp of red chilli powder (less if you don't like your food too spicy)
-1 tsp of something with a hint of acidity, either lemon juice, tamarind paste, white wine or cider vinegar, or amchur powder (dried unripe mango)
-2 tsps of salt, to taste
-1 finely sliced onion

Optional but recommended: A tsp of ground fenugreek (methi), a tsp of dried mint, half a tsp of dried coriander leaves, a finely sliced red onion to garnish

METHOD:

-Cube your potatoes then boil until they are cooked through but still have a little bit of bite. Take them out, drain, and put to the side.
-While the potatoes are cooling, get all your spices together and prepare your other ingredients.
-In a large pan, heat up two tbsps of oil to a medium heat. Add your cumin seeds if using and toast for a few seconds, add your ginger and garlic, chopped chillies, and stir for another thirty seconds.
-Add onion and soften.
-Add in your ground spices, stir thoroughly for a few seconds, then add in the potatoes and stir until they are covered in the spice mixture. Add salt. Add a touch more oil if the spices and potatoes are sticking to the bottom of the pan. Stir for up to five minutes.
-Add in your tsp of lemon juice, or tamarind, or vinegar, or amchur, and again stir thoroughly. Add red onion, mint, and coriander if using. Stir thoroughly.
-Serve, and enjoy!

Egg Curry

Here is a simple, quick, and tasty egg curry made with hard-boiled eggs. This is an excellent midweek meal with easily sourced ingredients, and not usually something people think of making. One of my favourites. You can also add frozen peas to this dish. The eggs don't freeze particularly well, but the sauce does so simply reheat and add more hard-boiled eggs.

INGREDIENTS:

-6 hard-boiled eggs
-2 400g tins of tomatoes
-1 tin of coconut milk
-1 tbsp of ginger garlic paste, or fresh equivalent
-1 bay leaf
-1/2 inch of cinnamon, or 1/2 a tsp of ground cinnamon
-2 green cardamom pod seeds, or 1/2 tsp of ground cardamom
-4 cloves
-2 tsps of garam masala
-1 tsp of ground fenugreek
-3 tsps of ground cumin
-2 tsps of ground coriander
-1 tsp of turmeric
-Salt to taste, about 2 tsps

METHOD:

-Bring water to a boil, then add in the eggs with shells on. Boil for seven minutes, take them out, and run a cold tap over them.
-Heat up a few tbsps of oil in a pot, add whole spices and stir for thirty seconds.
-Add onions and fry until they begin to turn golden.
-Add ginger garlic paste, fry for a further two minutes.
-Add ground spices, stir thoroughly for a minute.
-Add 400g tins of tomatoes and stir thoroughly, deglazing the pan.
-Simmer until this reduces by about a third.
-Reduce heat, add coconut milk and stir thoroughly. Simmer for a few minutes.
-Add in eggs, either whole or cut in half or quarters. Stir for a minute.
-Enjoy!

Fijian Potatoes

There is a very large South Asian diaspora in Fiji, most of them initially arrived as indentured workers brought over by the British to work on sugar cane plantations. This recipe comes from my mother's side of the family as my Mum was born in Lautoka on the island of Viti Levu to parents of Scottish and Australian descent. It is a great side dish that is tasty without being too fiery and is a wonderful accompaniment to most dishes.

INGREDIENTS:

-1 to 2 tsps of black or brown mustard seed (be careful as too many mustard seeds can make a dish very bitter)
-2 to 3 tbsps of oil, do not use olive oil. In fact, even rape seed oil is a bit heavy. I often use sunflower oil
-3 to 4 cloves
-4 to 5 whole green cardamom, crushed gently
-1 large onion, thinly sliced
-2 to 3 tsps of curry powder, any generic one will do. If you like your curries quite hot, you can add a little bit of chilli powder/cayenne
-10 curry leaves, fresh are best (they freeze very well) or dried are a good substitute
-750 g of potatoes, peeled and cut into 2-3 cm cubes (I always use Maris piper as they are floury and not waxy. King Edwards are a good alternative)

METHOD:

-Put the oil into a heavy bottomed pan and heat. Add the mustard seeds until they pop and change colour. Be careful not to burn them.
-Turn down the heat and add the curry leaves. Stir for about a minute. Add the cloves and cardamon and then the curry powder. Add onion.
-Gently fry until the onions are cooked. It often helps to put on the lid as this helps to slightly steam the onions
-Meanwhile, cook the potatoes in salted water until just cooked. Drain but keep a little of the cooking liquid. Be careful not to over cook as they can go a bit mushy.
-Add salt to the onion mixture and a little bit of oil or butter if needed as you need to be able to coat the potatoes with this.
-Add the potatoes and very carefully stir them until they are all covered on a low heat . You can use the same trick as when cooking pasta by adding a small amount of the cooking water. At this stage, you could add half a very thinly sliced raw onion and stir in. Turn off the heat and put on the lid. This gives everything a chance to infuse. It is best eaten warm and is great at a barbecue.

Flexitarian

A selection of adaptable recipes that can be made with meat or vegetables.

Tandoori/Tikka/Tikka Masala

The main difference between Tandoori and Tikka is that Tandoori is often made with larger pieces of meat on the bone or fish/vegetables/paneer, whereas Tikka is usually made with smaller portions of meat/fish/vegetables/paneer that are cubed and often on a skewer, and can be grilled. Both of these dishes are made from pre-marinating ingredients in a yoghurt paste with spices and are normally cooked in a traditional tandoor oven, but you can substitute with an oven and/or grill. This is a very versatile recipe as the paste is the same for meat/fish/vegetables/paneer. Only the marinating and cooking time will differ. The yoghurt, spices, marinating time and heat of the oven are key for making this work. You can also buy pre-made paste and mix this with yoghurt, but I find the taste is a lot more complex and fresher when made at home. Both of these are traditionally served like kebabs, without sauce, as a starter, main or side dish with rice, bread, chutneys, yoghurt, and pickles. Tikka Masala is a dish made from the marinated meat/fish/vegetables which are cooked in the oven/under the grill, then cooked further in and served with a creamy sauce, and there is some debate as to its origin. Though not too dissimilar from other Punjabi style butter chicken recipes, the generally accepted lore is that Tikka Masala originated in Glasgow when a chef improvised a new sauce by adding cream, tomato soup, and some spices to chicken that was sent back by a Glaswegian native for being too spicy, and a desire to eat meat with gravy.

There was even an attempt by MP Mohammed Sarwar to table a motion in the House of Commons for Glasgow to be given protected geographical status by the European Union for the creation of the Chicken Tikka Masala. In my opinion, it is a British dish, but specifically Scottish, by way of multiculturalism.

Ingredients for paste:

-400g Yoghurt
-3 tsp salt, preferably pink/Himalayan salt
-1 heaped tbsp ginger garlic paste
-1 heaped tsp ground cumin
-2 heaped tsp red chilli powder
-1 heaped tsp curry powder
-1 heaped tsp garam masala
-1 heaped tsp ground coriander
-1 heaped tsp of tamarind paste mixed with a little hot water, or juice from a lemon. You need some acidity to allow for the paste to work.
Optional: Red food colouring

Ingredients for sauce (optional):

-1 to 2 thinly sliced onions
-1 tbsp ginger garlic paste
-5 crushed cardamom pod seeds
-1 to 2 chopped chillies, to taste
-2 tsps of salt, to taste
-1 tsp cumin
-1 tsp ground coriander
-1 tsp turmeric
-1 tsp garam masala
-1 can of tinned tomatoes
-2 tbsps of ghee/butter/oil
-Heavy cream to taste
Optional: Cashew nuts blitzed in a food processor instead of cream.

METHOD:

-To make the paste, simply tip all of the spices and yoghurt into a large bowl and mix thoroughly for a few minutes.

-You can put your ingredients in from frozen, just don't put raw frozen meat and vegetables in the same bowl. For meat, you can use cubed lamb or chicken, or whole chicken breasts or thighs, or cubed fish or whole fillets. For a vegetarian version, potatoes, cauliflower, aubergine, peppers and paneer can be used.

-Place your ingredients in the marinade, meat and veg separately in separate containers/bowls, I like to use freezer bags, and leave for at least a few hours though overnight works best. Vegetables take less time to absorb flavours.

-If using cubes, it is best to use skewers to make small kebabs that can be held together, either way, take a baking tray, line with foil, and lay out your ingredients, shaking off any excess paste. If cooking vegetables you may want to put a little bit of oil on the foil to prevent drying out.

-Heat up your oven to at least 200C, up to 230C (390F to 450F, Gas Mark 4-6). Let this heat up over 10-15 minutes, ensuring the oven is really hot.

-The vegetables will only take about 15-30 minutes to cook, depending on size and what you are using, so check them regularly. You can then take them out and grill for a few minutes to crispen them on top.

-Meat will take longer, depending on whether you are using cubes or larger pieces, or meat on the bone. Large chicken breasts take about an hour to cook, turning halfway through then finishing up in the grill for 5 minutes. Make sure your meat is cooked through and turned halfway through cooking. If you are making a masala sauce they can be slightly undercooked as you will be finishing the meat in the sauce.

-If not making a masala sauce, simply serve and enjoy!

Optional Masala Sauce:

-Heat up onions in butter/ghee/oil and cook the onions until they turn very soft, add more oil if needed.
-Add whole spices if using.
-Add chilli and ginger garlic paste and cook for a further few minutes.
-Add tomato sauce or paste and cook until this forms a thick sauce.
-Let this simmer, adding a little water or stock if needed, until you are ready to put the meat/fish/vegetables in.
-If you have used large pieces of meat or whole fillets, now is a good time to chop these into chunks.
-Place your meat/fish/vegetables, stir in the sauce and cook for a few minutes, until cooked through if not completely cooked, otherwise enough to pick up the flavour of the sauce.
-Bring to a high heat, then simmer at a lower heat. Add in the cashews if using.
-At the lower heat, pour in the cream until you get the consistency/taste you want. The sauce will continue to thicken.
-Serve with rice and/or bread.
-Enjoy!

Korma

Here is a surprisingly easy and quick recipe for a restaurant quality korma that is ideal for both meat and vegetarian versions. You can use coconut milk to make this freezable and vegan, and/or soak a few handfuls of cashew nuts overnight then blend with water to make a sweet nutty paste to add towards the end of cooking time. If you are using cream use full fat so that it doesn't separate, you can use yoghurt if you want the sauce to be a bit lighter but that will also need to be full fat. Cream and yoghurt do not tend to freeze that well, though.

You can just use the ground spices and mango chutney to keep it simple, but I really like to add a bay leaf, crushed seeds from cardamom pods, cloves, a pinch of saffron and a stick of cinnamon for a wonderful depth of flavour that makes this recipe a cut above what you normally find.

INGREDIENTS:

-4 chicken breasts, or for a vegetarian version a mix of carrots, peas, mushrooms, pumpkin, sweetcorn, cauliflower, sweet potato, butternut squash, potatoes (though just about any veggies would work)
-300 ml of chicken or veg stock
-100ml of double cream, yoghurt, or coconut milk
-2 white onions, very finely chopped or even grated
-4 tsps of ginger garlic paste
-2 tbsps of mango chutney, or failing that two tsps of sugar
-2 heaped tsps of ground coriander
-2 heaped tsps of ground cumin
-1 heaped tsp of turmeric
-1/2 tsp of chilli powder
-2 tsbps vegetable oil/ghee/butter

Optional: 1 bay leaf, crushed seeds from 4 cardamom pods, 4 cloves, a pinch of saffron and a 2 inch single stick of cinnamon.

METHOD:

-If using chicken, cut into small cubes and season with black pepper, then fry this first in a little bit of oil until seared and mostly cooked. Take out of the pan and put to the side
-Fry your onion in a generous amount of butter/oil/ghee until they are very soft, about ten minutes, and stir occasionally. Add your ginger garlic paste, then fry for another minute. Add in whole spices (except saffron) if using and fry for a further minute.
-When the onions start to brown, put in your ground spices, add more oil if the onions starts to stuck to the bottom of the pan. Fry for a minute or two.
-Add in your stock and mango chutney, bring the mixture to a slight boil then back down to a simmer. Add saffron if using. Cook this for five minutes while stirring until the mixture reduces by half. You can at this point use a blender on the sauce to make it extra smooth. Add in vegetables that take a little longer to cook at this point, for example, pumpkin, butternut squash and potato and cook until halfway done.
-Add the rest of your vegetables at this point, if using chicken put this back in at this point as well. Add your cream/yoghurt/coconut milk/ almonds and stir through thoroughly. Cook for five to ten minutes, and check everything is cooked through. Remove cinnamon, bay leaves and cloves if used.
-You can garnish with a few cashew nuts or almonds, or coriander, or a few strands of saffron.
-Enjoy!

Jalfrezi

Jalfrezi comes from Bengal, and is a corruption of colloquial Bengali for spicy, jhal, and a Persian word, porhezi, which translates roughly to self-denial. Thus, this is a sauce that is hot, and also low calorie. During the British Raj, this sauce was also used as a way of cooking up any leftovers, so is incredibly versatile and can be used to curry just about anything, making it an ideal flexitarian recipe. I personally like to have this with paneer, but chicken and lamb also work very well.

If using paneer, soak your paneer in hot boiled water for at least ten minutes before adding in to the curry to cook for two minutes, or fry first for two minutes, then soak, then stir in at the end. Any colour of bell pepper will work, I like to use red or orange as they have a nice sweetness compared to the spiciness of the curry (I like this one particularly hot), though green also works brilliantly and is very popular, and a mixture of several is just wonderful.

INGREDIENTS:

-250g paneer/chicken
-1 tin of chopped tomatoes, or five freshly chopped tomatoes
-3 onions, white or red (I like to use a combination and a mix of finely chopped and roughly chopped for texture, flavour, and colour)
-1 to 2 bell peppers, any colour
-1 heaped tbsp of ginger garlic paste, or five cloves of garlic crushed and chopped and one inch of grated ginger (if you are using fresh ginger, feel free to add up to double this amount for more heat and tanginess)
-2 green chillies, finely chopped and/or two heaped tsps of chilli powder (reduce for less heat)
-1 heaped tsp of turmeric
-1 heaped tsp of cumin
-2 heaped tsps of garam masala

Optional but recommended: 1 tsp of white wine/cider vinegar or lemon juice, 1 tsp of ground fenugreek, freshly chopped coriander for garnish

METHOD:

-Fry then soak, or only soak your paneer in hot boiled water. This recipe also works particularly well with chicken and lamb, just season generously with pepper, fry whole spices first, then add in meat with the onions and ginger garlic and fry until golden brown, then add in tomatoes and ground spices and simmer for 10-20 minutes, then after checking the meat is cooked through, finally add in and cook peppers.
-Fry whole spices in oil if using, until aromas are released.
-Add in onions, fresh chillies if using, and ginger garlic paste. Fry until onions start to turn golden.
-Add in ground spices, stir thoroughly.
-Add in tomatoes, add half a cup to a cup of water, lower heat slightly and keep stirring until you get your desired consistency.
-Add in bell peppers and cook until tender, then add in paneer. If you haven't already fried the paneer cook this for two minutes. If you have fried the paneer first stir it in and garnish.
-Garnish with freshly chopped coriander if you have it, add in a tsp of vinegar or lemon juice and stir.
-Enjoy!

Biryani

Does this need an introduction? I'll give you one anyway. This is a good flexitarian recipe as you can easily make this vegetarian by substituting the meat for vegetables such as mushrooms, cauliflower, peas, aubergine, sweet potato, peppers, green beans, or carrots. You could even add hard boiled eggs in the rice. Even if you are not vegetarian you could also add vegetables in with the meat for a healthier and heartier meal. If you want your vegetables to be a bit firmer and still have bite add them in later by putting these on top of the rice for the last ten to fifteen minutes of cooking time. They will take less time to cook than the meat, and make sure to check everything is thoroughly cooked through at the end. Or just marinate everything that you want to use together and follow the recipe, making sure the meat is cooked through. Some people like to add raisins and/or nuts on top of the rice. You will need to use full fat yoghurt for the marinade so that this does not burn or separate when cooking. If you don't do lactose and/or wish to make this vegan, skip the marinating step and cook your ingredients in a pan for a few minutes with onion and the spices listed in the marinade and ginger garlic, then add half a cup of vegetable stock when layering in the pot, add mostly cooked rice on top, and cook for 20 minutes in the oven You can also marinade in soy-based yoghurt products, and shake off the excess before cooking in the pot.

I often use chopped chicken breast fillets they are readily available and take less time to cook, though this is traditionally made with chicken on the bone and a mixture of legs, thighs, and breasts. This recipe also works for lamb or even beef, venison, or goat, just you may need to cook this for a bit longer. The easiest way to make this is to marinate your ingredients before, then half cook the rice with spices, then layer the meat then rice and/or vegetables in a large casserole dish, roasting tray, baking tray, Dutch oven or similar (as long as you can add a lid or cover with foil), then put everything in the oven. You can cook this on the stove, but you will need to add a cup of stock until your ingredients are just covered, then rice, and cook on a medium heat with a lid on tightly until everything is cooked through, the cooking time will be the same. Oven is definitely best if you can.

The thing is, Biryanis are incredibly popular across South Asia, the diaspora, and beyond so there are many, many variations and many, many more strongly held opinions on what constitutes and belongs in a Biryani. The origins of this dish are within the Muslim population of South Asia, and there are many styles within this region and beyond in Western Asia, Afghanistan, Indonesia, Myanmar, the Philippines, South Africa, Thailand, Mauritius, Malaysia, and Singapore, as well as many other countries that the South Asian diaspora have moved to. This dish was initially brought to the South Asian region from Persia through the Mughal empire, and is probably the most well-known dish from Mughal cuisine and a classic example of 'dum' cooking, in which ingredients are marinated first and then slow cooked together in a tightly sealed pot for maximum flavour.

INGREDIENTS:

Marinade:
-2 heaped tbsps of ginger garlic paste
-1 tbsp of garam masala
-1 heaped tsp of salt
-1 heaped tsp of turmeric
-1 heaped tsp of ground cumin
-1 heaped tsp of ground coriander
-1 heaped tsp of chilli powder
-3 tbsps of full fat yoghurt, enough to cover the ingredients but not so that they are swimming in yoghurt

Rice:
-4 bay leaves
-6 cloves
-6 cardamom pods, crushed and shells removed so only the seeds are used
-2 to 3 inch stick of cinnamon
-2 tsps of cumin seeds
-1 tsp of turmeric
-2 tbsps of salt (less if you are using stock)

Other: 3 white onions, thinly sliced and fried until crispy

Optional: Mint leaves, coriander leaves, saffron water, chopped chillies

METHOD:

-Roughly chop your main ingredients for the biryani, whether meat or veg. For this recipe I often use four large chicken breasts cut into large chunks, you can also use whole legs or thighs, or beef or lamb, but these will take longer to cook. Add the spices from the marinade, then add yoghurt so there is enough to cover the ingredients but not drown them. Mix thoroughly and marinate for at least twenty minutes to overnight.
-Finely slice your onions and fry until brown and crispy.
-Measure out two cups of rice, rinse until the water runs clear then soak for 30 minutes in two cups of warm water. Rinse again.
-Bring water to the boil, add rice and spices together and cook until rice is 50% to 60% done. Drain and remove whole spices if you wish.
-Remove the bits of meat and/or vegetables from the marinade and shake off any excess, then add to the bottom of the pot. If using fried onions and chillies, add half of this too. You can simmer this for a minute if you wish.
-Layer on your half-cooked rice, then add the rest of the onion, chilli, chopped coriander, and chopped mint if using. If you want you can also add a tbsp of hot water to some saffron strands and add this for added colour/flavour. Cover with foil or a lid.
-Put in the oven at 190C/Gas Mark 5 for 30 minutes for vegetables, 45 minutes for chicken breasts, 1 hour for chicken on the bone/lamb. Check everything is cooked through before serving.
-Enjoy!

Dum Curry

An excellent dish from Mughal cuisine, this recipe is particularly easy as you just briefly fry your ingredients, mix them together, and shove them in the oven. Despite using very few spices and ingredients it is also very tasty. Based on Dum cooking, which would have been done in a large clay pot over a fire, this is a great meal to make using a casserole dish, particularly if it is flame proof as then this becomes a one pot recipe.

You could turn this into a biryani if you wish by half cooking your rice with spices then laying it on top, but you can also just cook rice separately, or eat this as a stew. I think it goes particularly well with rice cooked with a tsp of turmeric and a tsp of cumin seeds. You can easily make this vegetarian, by substituting the meat as described in the ingredients, and adjust the cooking time to about 30 minutes.

INGREDIENTS:

-500g of stewing beef, or stewing lamb (you could also get a cheap cut of meat and cut it into chunks yourself. Because you are cooking it for a long time in liquid this works well with cheap meat). For vegetarians mushrooms, cauliflower, peas, aubergine, sweet potato, peppers, green beans, or carrots would work well, just about anything to be honest
-3 to 4 onions, any colour, finely chopped
-1 heaped tbsp of garam masala, or your favourite curry powder
-2 heaped tbsps of ginger garlic paste, or a whole garlic with cloves crushed and chopped, and 2 inches of grated ginger
-2 tsps of salt
-2 tsps of ground black pepper
-4 heaped tbsps of yoghurt (full fat so it doesn't separate, if it's the solid kind you will need to stir it for a bit so it becomes a liquid)

Optional: 1 tsp of chilli powder for a bit of a kick, or 2 chopped chillies, chopped coriander for garnishing with

METHOD:

-Preheat your oven to 180C/Gas Mark 4.
-Fry your meat or vegetables for a few minutes in a touch of oil, if using meat make sure it is browned on all sides. Remove from the pot and put aside.
-Add your onions, fry until they turn soft, five to ten minutes. Add ginger garlic, fry for another minute. Add spices and salt, fry for another minute.
-Lower the heat and add yoghurt, add main ingredients, stir and simmer for a minute making sure everything is coated.
-Transfer to an oven proof dish, if you are not using one already, then cover with a lid or foil. Cook in the oven for an hour and a half until the meat is tender. If the meat is still a bit tough add in a cup of stock and return to the oven for twenty to thirty minutes.
-Enjoy!

Keema Mattar

This was the first curry I learned to cook and sustained me throughout university. It was also the first meal I ever made for my husband, so it has a special place in my heart. I have tweaked it over the years, I used to cook it using only ginger, garlic, and the spices listed in the main ingredient list as that is what was cheap and what I could easily get, but I would recommend adding as many of the optional but recommended as possible for a wonderful depth of flavour.

INGREDIENTS:

-1kg of mince, I prefer lamb but you can use any minced meat or vegetarian/vegan mince
-5 onions, white or red, finely chopped
-1 garlic, cloves crushed and chopped
-2 inches of grated ginger
-1 400g tin of tomatoes
-4 heaped tsps of ground cumin
-4 heaped tsps of ground coriander
-1 heaped tsp of turmeric
-1 heaped tbsp of garam masala or curry powder
-2 tsps of chilli powder, less if you don't like your food too spicy
-1 tbsp of salt
-1 tsp of ground pepper

Optional but highly recommended: 5 cloves, 3 bay leaves, 1 tsp of ground cinnamon, 2 heaped tsps of tamarind paste, 1 heaped tsp of ground fenugreek (methi)

METHOD:

-Fry your onions until soft, about 10 minutes.
-Add ginger and garlic, stir for a minute.
-Add in any whole spices and stir thoroughly.
-Add in your mince and cook until brown or nearly cooked.
-Add in ground spices.
-Add in tinned tomatoes, add tamarind paste if using, add salt.
-Simmer for 40 minutes, adding more water and salt if needed but you want this to be a dry curry.
-Add in peas, and sprinkle an extra half tsp of ground coriander and ground cumin each, cook through.
-Garnish with chopped coriander leaves of you have them, taste test if you need more salt, then serve.
-Enjoy!

Achari

This is a particularly versatile sauce that can be vegan, vegetarian, or made with meat. Some people add a little yoghurt to the sauce before serving, but I like to keep it plain to really taste the spicy, sweet, and sour flavours together. Plus, the colour is just fabulous.

This also happens to be extremely easy as a recipe. Achar is the Hindi/Urdu word for pickle, and the main flavours of this recipe come from pickles, mango and lime in this case, and a tbsp of Panch Phoron which you can also substitute with any curry powder or garam masala.

Most pickles contain the seeds in Panch Phoron which means you can substitute the panch phoron with curry powder.

INGREDIENTS:

-500g of any meat and/or vegetables. This works well with mushrooms, aubergine, carrots, radish, potatoes, green beans, peas, cauliflower, and paneer. For meat use diced chicken, lamb, or beef
-3 onions, white or red, finely chopped
-1 heaped tbsp of ginger garlic paste, or 5 cloves of garlic cloves crushed and chopped, and 1 inch of grated ginger
-1 400g tin of tomatoes
-1 tbsp of mango chutney, chop up any big bits
-1 tbsp of lime pickle, chop up any big bits
-1 tbsp of panch phoron, or curry powder, or garam masala, or a tsp each of black pepper, cumin, garam masala, ground coriander, turmeric, fenugreek, and garam masala each
-Salt and pepper to taste

Optional: 1 bay leaf, yoghurt stirred in just before serving, chopped coriander for garnish

METHOD:

-Heat up a little oil in to a pan, add your whole spices and toast for a minute, stirring frequently so that they don't burn.
-Add in your onions and ginger garlic. Cook until they start to soften.
-Add in your meat and cook for five to ten minutes, or vegetables and cook until almost done but still tender, if you are cooking both together brown your meat first.
-Add in chopped tomatoes and chutneys, add two tsps of salt and a touch of ground pepper.
-Simmer for twenty minutes, adding only a touch of water if needed. Keep cooking until your ingredients are cooked through/you have the consistency you desire.
-If using yoghurt, lower the heat first then stir in. Garnish with chopped coriander if you have it.
-Enjoy!

Rogan Josh

There is a little debate as to where the name originates from, 'Roughan' in Urdu translates to oil or butter and 'ghosht' means lamb, thus meaning meat stewed in butter which is how the dish is made. This dish also has a distinctive red colour to the oil and sauce, and originally this colour would come from using the Alkanna tinctoria flower, also known as the dyer's alkanet, of which the roots produce a bright red colour when crushed. This could be another origin of the Rogan Josh name, as the flower's Urdu name is Ratan Jot. These days the colour comes from using Kashmiri chillies, or red chilli powder.

This is a good recipe for people who do not eat onion or garlic, as traditionally this would be made with a tbsp of fennel seeds, and a tsp of hing/asafoetida which are also wonderful substitutes for onions and garlic in most curries. This dish originates from Kashmir, and Kashmiri versions of this recipe do not contain tomatoes, onion, or garlic despite them being a popular addition elsewhere. It is believed the inclusion of onion, garlic, and tomatoes was as a result of Punjabi influence when this dish was brought there by the Mughals. If you must add tomatoes, add them after the meat and cook for a while so the acidity and flavour is reduced before adding the yoghurt. If you don't have fresh ginger or garlic, use two tbsps of ginger garlic paste.

This recipe is relatively easy, there is a bit of cooking at the beginning then you can just leave the covered pot on the stove on a very low heat for at least an hour and a half or so while checking occasionally, I often like to do this instead of a roast on Sundays. This does taste best when left to simmer for as long as possible. You want to cook this until a thick layer of red oil separates from the sauce and the meat is incredibly tender, and falls apart at the slightest touch. If I'm using lamb, I often have this simmering at a very low heat for up to three hours. For a vegetarian version substitute the meat with a mix of aubergine, cauliflower, carrots, and potatoes, and simmer until cooked through. For a vegan version, substitute the yoghurt with a 400g tin of tomatoes. This recipe is particularly excellent with Indian breads as you can pick up the bits of delicious meat and/or vegetables.

INGREDIENTS:

-1kg of meat, or veg, diced into chunks
-400g of full fat yoghurt
-1 garlic, cloves crushed and chopped
-1 inch of grated ginger
-2 onions
-5 heaped tbsps of ghee, or 8 to 10 tbsps of oil
-2 inches of cinnamon stick, or one tsp of ground cinnamon
-8 cardamom pods, crush and use the seeds, discard the pods
-6 cloves
-3 bay leaves
-2 tsps of cumin, seeds or ground cumin
-2 to three tsps of red chilli powder
-1 tbsp of ground coriander
-2 tsps of garam masala

Optional but recommended: Seeds from 2 black cardamom pods, 2 tsps of fennel seeds, generous pinch of saffron strands

METHOD:

-Heat oil in a pot to a low medium heat, crush your whole spices a bit by either using a mortar and pestle, or put them in a freezer bag and crush them using a heavy object, then put in the oil and stir for a minute.
-If using onions, put them in the pot and cook for about five minutes, add ginger garlic, cook for another few minutes.
-Add in your meat and brown for ten minutes, then reduce heat. Add ground spices and stir so that the meat is covered.
-Stir your yoghurt to remove any lumps, then add to the meat a bit at a time while stirring. Add saffron if using. Cook for a few minutes.
-Put a lid on the pan, or cover with foil and leave to simmer on a low heat for an hour and a half to two hours at least, checking occasionally that it is not sticking to the pan. Add a touch of water or more oil if this happens.
-When nearly cooked, add two tsps of salt and a tsp of ground pepper, or more to taste. Cook for a further five minutes.
-Take out your bits of meat, garnish with freshly chopped coriander if you have it, and serve with rice and/or chapati.
-Enjoy!

Bhuna

You will find a bhuna on almost every restaurant menu. Bhuna refers to the tempering of spices in oil at the start of cooking. This recipe is very simple, has few ingredients, and a well-rounded flavour. The spices are very similar to the curry sauce I make and freeze in advance so following that recipe makes an excellent bhuna sauce you can use at a later date. The bhuna is characterised by a thick sauce made from onions and tomatoes. Easy to make vegan, vegetarian, as well as with any meat.

INGREDIENTS:

-500g meat or vegetables
-3 onions, finely chopped
-1 400g tin of tomatoes
-1 heaped tbsp of ginger garlic paste, or equivalent fresh
-2 heaped tsps of garam masala
-2 heaped tsps of ground cumin
-2 heaped tsps of ground coriander
-1 heaped tsp of turmeric
-1 to two tsps of chilli powder, or one to two green chillies, to taste
-2 tsps of salt, to taste
-2 tbsps of oil/ghee

Optional: a touch of lemon juice, 1 tsp of methi, added salt, 1 tsp of garam masala to finish

METHOD:

-Heat oil in a pan to a medium heat.
-Add in spices, stir for thirty seconds.
-Add ginger garlic paste, stir for thirty seconds.
-Add in onions, make sure nothing is sticking to the bottom of the pan. Add a touch more oil or water is this happens.
-Add salt.
-Stir onions until they soften.
-Add in your main ingredient, stir for five minutes. If using meat, you want to cook until browned slightly.
-Add in your 400g tin of tomatoes, if you want a thicker more liquid sauce add half a mug of water.
-Simmer for 30 minutes, stirring occasionally.
-Add a touch of lemon juice and more salt to taste, if you wish.
-Serve with rice and/or chapati.
-Enjoy!

Madras

The Madras curry as it is known in the UK is a British Indian restaurant invention (particularly British Bangladeshi owned Indian restaurants) and doesn't really exist outside this sphere. It is not particularly similar to any curry found in Madras, which is now named Chennai. This is a very spicy, aromatic, and tangy curry. Not for the faint of heart!

If you don't like your food too hot, reduce the chilli powder and/or add coconut milk, and/or serve with yoghurt. This is a very simple, quick, easy, and versatile curry that is ideal for midweek cooking and freezes well. Serve with rice and/or chapati, and if you wish a dash of yoghurt and mango chutney.

This is an excellent flexitarian recipe as you can use this sauce to curry anything you like, be it meat, veg, or even pulses. For pulses you will need to add a few cups of water until the lentils are covered, and add two tsps of salt, then bring to the boil and simmer until they are tender.

There are many Madras curry powders you can buy that contain the spices below, and if you want to make life a bit easier I find that a tbsp of this works well in most cases. I have found that the key to this dish, whether you are using curry powder or not, is to add at least one tbsp of some acidity, be it white wine vinegar, tamarind, or lemon juice.

INGREDIENTS:

-1kg of meat, veg, or two cups of pulses
-4 onions
-2 heaped tbsps of ginger garlic paste, or fresh equivalent
-2 400g tins of tomatoes
-2 tsps of garam masala
-3 heaped tsps of cumin, seeds or ground cumin
-3 heaped tsps of ground coriander
-2 heaped tsps of chilli powder, or 3 to 4 chopped chillies
-1 heaped tsp of turmeric
-1 bay leaf
-2 tbsps of white wine vinegar, or 1 tbsp of tamarind or lemon juice
-Salt and ground black pepper to taste
-2 tbsp of oil

Optional but recommended: 8 to 10 curry leaves and/or freshly chopped coriander, 1 tsp of mustard seed, 2 tsps of ground fenugreek (methi), a few peppercorns instead of ground pepper

METHOD:

-Pour a generous glug of oil in to a pot and heat up to a low to medium heat.
-Add in any whole spices you are using and toast for thirty seconds.
-Add in your onions, ginger, garlic and fresh chillies if using.
-Turn up the heat slightly and cook until the onions soften.
-Add in your ground spices and stir thoroughly. Add a little dash more oil or water if this sticks to the bottom of the pan.
-Add in your ingredients, meat/veg/lentils, and stir thoroughly so that they are coated in the onions and spices. For meat you want to do this until the meat browns, for vegetables you want to stir for a few minutes, and for lentils a minute at most.
-Add in your 400g tins of tomatoes and stir thoroughly. If you haven't used peppercorns, add two tsps of ground pepper. Add two tsps of salt.
-Keep your curry simmering for thirty minutes, stirring occasionally.
-Check the salt and spice levels, adding more to your taste if needed.
-Add in a tbsp of white wine vinegar. If using lemon juice or tamarind, add one tbsp. Lower the heat.
-Garnish with freshly chopped coriander if using.
-Enjoy!

Pathia

This sweet, sour, and spicy curry has its origins in Persia yet has found a home as a firm favourite in the British Indian curry houses. It was brought to India by the Parsi people, who originate from Iran but have been settled in India since the 8th Century. It is always worth bearing in mind that Indian cuisine has always been continuously adapted and exchanged with the many different cultural influences that have formed the history and identities of the South Asian subcontinent, and beyond.

After a bit of experimentation, the key to getting that particular balance and depth of flavour is to use tamarind rather than vinegar or lime juice as some recipes suggest. For the sweetness jaggery (Indian style cane sugar) works best, though brown sugar is a close second. If you don't have either jaggery or brown sugar, a touch of mango chutney or honey would also work, or two tsps of white sugar. If you don't have curry leaves, use two bay leaves. You can also make this dish without ginger if you can't find any.

Like most of the dishes here, this is a flexitarian recipe that can be used to curry vegetable, meat, or fish/seafood dishes depending on what you have available and your dietary requirements. I do however really recommend prawns and/or fish with this sauce.

INGREDIENTS:

-500g of meat, fish/seafood, or vegetables
-4 finely chopped onions
-1 400g tin of tomatoes
-1 tbsp of garlic paste, or one entire garlic with the cloves crushed and chopped finely, and if you wish, an inch of grated ginger, or one heaped tbsp of ginger garlic paste (ginger is optional for this recipe)
-1 400g tin of tomatoes
-1 bay leaf
-2 heaped tsps of garam masala
-2 heaped tsps of ground cumin
-2 heaped tsps of ground coriander
-2 tsps of red chilli powder and/or freshly chopped chillies to taste
-2 tsps of salt to taste
-1 tbsp of tamarind paste
-2 heaped tsps of brown sugar/jaggery, or one tbsp of honey or one tbsp of mango chutney
-2 tbsp of oil

Optional but highly recommended: 2 heaped tsps of ground fenugreek (methi), 6 to 8 curry leaves

METHOD:

-Heat up a generous amount of oil to medium heat in a pan, add your garlic (and ginger if using) and fry for a few seconds.
-Add your powdered spices and stir for a few seconds. If they stick to the bottom of the pan add a touch of water or more oil. Stir thoroughly until you get a paste.
-Add in your finely chopped onion and stir thoroughly. Add fresh chillies if using. Cook until they start to turn soft.
-Add in your main ingredients. If using meat you want to brown this, if using vegetables fry for a few minutes. If anything starts to stick at the bottom of the pan add a touch of water. If using seafood put this in at a later point.
-Add your tomatoes, bay leaves, curry leaves, and salt. Simmer for twenty minutes.
-Add in your tamarind and sugar. Simmer for a further ten minutes. If using seafood add this after simmering. Make sure everything is cooked through before serving.
-Garnish with freshly chopped coriander if you wish. Serve with rice and/or chapati.
-Enjoy!

Vindaloo

The origins of the Vindaloo can be traced back to Portugal. It is thought that the name comes from 'vin' referring to wine, and 'aloo' being Hindi for potatoes, but in fact this is a corruption of a Portuguese dish 'Carne de vinha d'alhos', which is meat in a wine marinade. The Vindaloo is an Indian version of this, and comes from Goa which was the centre of the Portuguese colony in India. This particular recipe is from my dad and is one of his favourites. I tend to make this with pork as that is the most traditional version, but I also add a few potatoes.

If you are making this vegetarian, marinade all your ingredients together then cook in the oven/on the stove for thirty to forty minutes. If you are doing a mix of meat and vegetables, marinade your meat, cook for thirty minutes then add vegetables for the last thirty minutes. I highly recommend potatoes. Serve with rice. Have yoghurt or raita on the side if you don't like it too spicy, or reduce the chilli powder. This is a hot dish!

INGREDIENTS:

-1 kg of diced meat or vegetables (if using meat, also add three to four potatoes)
-2 tins of coconut milk
-3 to 4 onions
-3 inches of grated ginger, one whole garlic cloves crushed and finely chopped (if using ginger garlic paste, use 2 heaped tbsps)
-5 tbsps of white wine vinegar
-1 tbsp of ground cumin
-1 tbsp of ground coriander
-1 tbsp of turmeric
-1 tbsp of red chilli powder
-1 tbsp of salt
-2 tsps of ground black pepper
-1 tbsp of mustard seed

METHOD:

-Preheat oven to 190C/Gas Mark 4. Mix all your ground spices, salt, pepper, and vinegar into a paste. Add in your meat/vegetables and stir thoroughly. If you are cooking meat and potatoes/vegetables together, only marinade the meat and add potatoes/vegetables later. Put this to the side while you prep your onions, ginger and garlic. You can leave this overnight, but I find simply leaving it while I get everything else ready is enough.

-Heat oil/ghee in a pot. Add mustard seeds and cook for thirty seconds until they are dancing. Add onions and fry until turning golden. Add ginger garlic and fry for a further minute.

-Add in your meat/vegetables and fry for five minutes.

-Add in coconut milk and stir thoroughly. Simmer for a minute.

-Add lid and put in the oven or cook on a low heat for half an hour for vegetables, an hour for meat, and if adding veg put this in halfway through.

-Enjoy!

Desserts / Sweets

Something sweet for a treat.

Kheer (Rice Pudding)

You can freeze rice pudding, just ensure that it is in a completely sealed container and you eat it within a month. Defrost in the fridge first, then eat it cold or microwave to heat up first.

This is one of my childhood favourites. You can make this using only rice, milk, and sugar. Popular things to add are saffron, cardamom, cinnamon, vanilla extract, and even nuts and fruit. I like to add cardamom, cinnamon and saffron for a richer colour and flavour. Super easy to make, and you can do it over the stove or finish up in the oven.

INGREDIENTS:

-Rice, ½ a mug, any kind though pudding rice works best
-Whole milk, 1 litre
-Sugar, 4 tbsps

Optional: Saffron (just a pinch), cardamom seeds (from 3 or 4 pods), cinnamon (1 to 2 inch stick), vanilla extract (1 tsp), nuts, fruit. If using ground cinnamon or cardamom use 1 tsp, to taste, and use either cardamom or vanilla extract, not both at the same time

METHOD:

-Rinse your rice, then soak for 30 minutes. Drain.
-If you are using cardamom seeds, add these to the drained rice then toast it all in a large pan for a minute until the rice loses excess moisture and the aromas are released.
-Add milk and put on a medium to high heat and stir regularly until the milk boils and froths up to the top of the pan. This will take a while, then happen very suddenly after 10 or so minutes so watch carefully.
-Lower the heat, add in your cinnamon and saffron if using. Add sugar.
-Keep cooking at a lower temperature, stirring every two minutes or so for the next 30 minutes until the rice is thoroughly cooked, and both the rice and mixture thicken to your desired consistency. Or put in a preheated oven at 140C/Gas Mark One for an hour. Once cooked add any nuts and/or fruit.
-Enjoy!

Chai Masala Cupcakes And Buttercream Icing

What is a better treat than cupcakes? Cupcakes made with chai!

INGREDIENTS:

For the batter:
-110g/4oz butter or margarine, softened at room temperature
-110g/4oz caster sugar
-2 free-range eggs, lightly beaten
-1 tsp vanilla extract
-110g/4oz self-raising flour
-1-2 tbsp chai (see chai recipe in snacks section).

For the buttercream icing:
-140g/5oz butter, softened
-280g/10oz icing sugar
-1-2 tbsp chai (see chai recipe in snacks section)
- A few drops of food colouring, or sprinkles, or a little bit of powdered cinnamon for decoration

METHOD:

-Preheat the oven to 180C/350F/Gas 4.
-Cream the butter and sugar for the batter recipe together in a bowl until pale. Beat in the eggs a little at a time.
-Fold in the flour using a large metal spoon, adding a little milk until the mixture is of a dropping consistency. Spoon the mixture into paper cases until they are half full.
-Bake in the oven for 10-15 minutes, or until golden-brown on top and a skewer inserted into one of the cakes comes out clean. Set aside to cool for 10 minutes, then remove from the tin and cool on a wire rack.
-Decorate as you see fit. For the buttercream icing, beat the butter in a large bowl until soft. Add half the icing sugar and beat until smooth.
-Then add the remaining icing sugar with one tbsp of the chai, adding more if necessary, until the mixture is smooth and creamy. You can also add sprinkles, or a touch of ground cinnamon.
-Enjoy!

Anzac Biscuits

This is a very simple recipe that makes tasty biscuits that also last for ages. My maternal grandmother was Australian, so these were a childhood favourite. Named after the Australian and New Zealand Army Corps, they are firmly associated with Anzac Day which is a national day of remembrance in Australia and New Zealand which commemorates Australians and New Zealanders who have served and died in combat. This takes place on the 25th April, the date of the first engagement of the ANZAC corps in the First World War, in Gallipoli.

There is a little bit of debate as to the origin of the recipe, some believe that the biscuits were sent over from Australia and New Zealand by wives and women's groups to troops serving abroad, as they keep for a relatively long time, and others believe that they were used to raise money back home for the war through bake sales. It could also be both!

INGREDIENTS:

-100g plain flour
-100g caster sugar
-100g butter, plus greasing
-85g of dessicated coconut
-85g porridge oats
-1 tbsp golden syrup
-1 tbsp boiling water
-1tsp bicarbonate of soda

METHOD:

-Preheat oven to 160C/Gas Mark 3-4.
-Combine dry ingredients into a bowl.
-Melt butter and golden syrup, either on the stove or in the microwave.
-Stir bicarbonate of soda in the boiling water then add to syrup and butter.
-Pour butter, golden syrup, bicarbonate of soda and water in to dry. ingredients and stir until mixed through.
-Place tsps of mixture on to a lightly greased baking tray, taking care to distance the biscuits to allow for spreading. Flatten slightly.
-Bake for 15 minutes, slightly less if you prefer them chewy. Loosen while still slightly warm, then cool on trays or racks.
-Enjoy!

Dream Bars

This was my favourite treat growing up, and I have very fond memories of making these with my mum as a child.

These cakes are absolutely delicious, easy, and incredibly rich. If you love chocolate and coconut they are a must-have, and I find that they go down very easily as a mid-afternoon snack with a cup of tea, or even as a dessert with some ice cream. My mum and I always called these dream bars, and I am sure if you try them you will see why!

INGREDIENTS:

Cakes:

-155g of plain flour
-125g of sugar
-90g desiccated coconut
-1 tbsp of cocoa
-185g of butter
-1/2 tsp of vanilla extract
-1 egg

Icing:

-185g icing sugar
-2 tbsps cocoa
-30g butter
-1 and a half tbsps hot water
-Desiccated coconut for decorating

METHOD:

-Sift dry cake ingredients into a bowl.
-Add melted butter, vanilla, and egg. Mix well.
-Press mixture into a greased baking tray, preferably 28cm x 18cm.
-Bake at 160C/Gas Mark 3 for 15 minutes.
-Take out and let it cool.
-Make the icing by sifting cocoa and sugar into a bowl, add melted butter and water, and stir until smooth and glossy.
-When the cake mixture is cold, ice and decorate with coconut.
-Cut into bars when the icing has set.
-Enjoy!

Printed in Poland
by Amazon Fulfillment
Poland Sp. z o.o., Wrocław

62716732R00112